# Grandma's
# Best Recipes

# Grandma's
# Best Recipes

Traditional comfort food

just like Grandma used to make

This edition published in 2010

LOVE FOOD is an imprint of Parragon Books Ltd

Parragon
Queen Street House
4 Queen Street
Bath BA1 1HE, UK

Copyright © Parragon Books Ltd 2007

LOVE FOOD and the accompanying heart device is a registered trade mark of Parragon
Books Ltd in Australia, the UK, USA, India and the EU

ISBN 978-1-4454-0872-9

Internal design by Jane Bozzard-Hill
Photography by Clive Bozzard-Hill
Home economists: Sandra Baddeley and Valerie Barrett
Introduction by Pamela Gwyther

Printed in China

**Notes for the reader**
This book uses metric and imperial measurements. Follow the same units of measurement
throughout; do not mix metric and imperial. All spoon measurements are level, unless
otherwise stated; teaspoons are assumed to be 5 ml, and tablespoons are assumed to be
15 ml. Unless otherwise stated, milk is assumed to be whole, eggs and individual fruits,
such as bananas, are medium, and pepper is freshly ground black pepper.

Recipes using raw or lightly cooked eggs should be avoided by infants, the elderly,
pregnant women, convalescents and anyone suffering from an illness. Pregnant and
breast-feeding women are advised to avoid eating peanuts and peanut products.

# CONTENTS

# INTRODUCTION

*This is a book about all of our favourite childhood food memories, and it will give you the opportunity to create dishes 'just like Grandma used to make'. It will conjure up all the wonderful food smells that would always be present when we went to visit our grandparents as children, and the warm home-cooked meals that were waiting for us. It would be particularly welcoming to arrive when Grandma had just been baking and there was a selection of cakes and biscuits, and even freshly baked bread to smother with butter and eat fresh from the oven. Grandma's food was always a comfort; just the right thing to cheer you up, soothe a cold or even help heal a broken heart. Like Grandma herself, her food was always there and could be relied upon in all circumstances.*

## 'Grandma's food was always a comfort – just the thing to cheer you up'

For many of us, our childhoods were very much linked to our grandparents. When we visited them for Christmas and other holidays, all the traditional foods would appear as if by magic. It is only with hindsight that we appreciate the amount of planning and hard work that went into making our perfect holidays. Often we would not only be able to eat the food but also have the thrill of helping to make it. Somehow, Grandma always had time to allow us to roll out the pastry and biscuits and help mix the cakes. She even allowed us to lick the wooden spoon and scrape the mixing bowl to try the delicious mix before it went in the oven. It was here that many of us learned to cook as Grandma was able to spend time with us and pass on the considerable knowledge that she had acquired over the years.

Weekends spent at our grandparents' often meant a traditional roast would be served. In addition to a huge joint of meat, there would be all the accompaniments: the vegetables, roast potatoes and parsnips, oodles of gravy and always Yorkshire pudding, even when it wasn't beef. The meal would always be followed by a wonderful pudding – apple pie, rhubarb crumble or maybe a lemon meringue pie. When there was a celebration, like a birthday, there might even be a Black Forest gateau or an iced cake with candles for the birthday girl or boy to blow out.

The food Grandma prepared for everyday meals was simpler. Firstly, because times were harder in her day, the maximum use was made of leftovers, such as shepherd's pie and bubble and squeak using the remnants from the Sunday roast. Meals tended to be rather heavy as people often had to do more physical work and didn't have cars, so would walk relatively long distances. Casseroles and stews using the cheaper cuts of meat were prepared and cooked for a long time in a slow oven so that the meat would be really tender. Sausages and potatoes were also popular as they were filling and economical. Vegetables were often home-grown so they were fresh and in season. Some of the surplus vegetable and fruits would be preserved for use later in the year – fruit was turned into jam and vegetables were salted or made into chutneys.

Today's generation of grandmothers is more likely to be engaged full-time in the workplace and trying to juggle home, family, work, hobbies, interests and travels abroad. Her time for cooking has been reduced and she probably saves the traditional foods for special occasions and chooses quicker and healthier recipes in her day-to-day cooking. Her food habits are changing too, influenced by travel to far-away places and sampling the local fare. Today's multicultural society also means

*'Like Grandma herself, her food could be relied upon
in all circumstances'*

that we eat different foods on different occasions and celebrate new festivals. We also have a wider variety of food ingredients available, making many exciting new recipes and exotic meals far more accessible.

As the years have passed, our eating habits have changed. Foods that would have been considered exotic twenty years ago have become part of our everyday life – and comfort foods in their own right. Chicken tikka masala has overtaken roast beef as our nation's favourite dish. Pizza is another example of a food which has been absorbed into our national food identity along with others, such as chicken Kiev, spaghetti Bolognese and chilli con carne. This is a result of the changing population of our own country and the fact that many of us now have the opportunity to travel throughout the world. Most of our grandparents did not get the chance to journey much further than their own backyards, but global travel has widened the range of food experiences for today's generation. South American, Asian and Eastern European foods have all become part of our regular diet in recent years.

The way we eat has also changed through recent years. Although many will say that it is a shame that families tend not to sit down together for meals anymore, some food habits have changed for the better. We eat a lighter diet and consume more good-quality fresh fruits and vegetables now that these are available throughout the year. We are much more aware of what foods are good for us, although our busy lifestyles often lead us to make unwise food choices and to give in to the convenience of ready-made food or takeaways.

Obviously at the weekends, when we have more time, the favourite recipes come into their own. Although they may have a newer twist or include a prepared ingredient, like ready-to-use pastry, they are essentially the foods we ate in our childhood. Also, when there is a birthday or anniversary we tend to make more of an effort in preparing the food and are more extravagant with its selection. This is also the time when we might bake, providing family or friends with something delicious, like gingerbread or coffee and walnut cake, to accompany a cup of tea or coffee. Some people spend some of their time at weekends preparing home-cooked food and then freezing it for later in the week. In order to do this you need to be organised and have large saucepans so that you can make dishes in large quantities, but it is worth the effort.

*Comfort foods are the old favourites: the meals that are particularly familiar to us, give us a warm feeling and soothe our souls. Grandma made these for us when we were young, so the good feelings associated with them are still there. When we are upset, worried or depressed, simple food like a warming chicken or tomato soup is just what is needed. Dishes that you can eat with your hands, such as a grilled cheese sandwich or a tasty hamburger, are just the thing when you don't feel like sitting at the table with a*

# GRANDMA'S COMFORT FOOD

*knife and fork. A casserole is an excellent standby for a cold winter's day and provides a great opportunity to get the family sitting around the table, eating and discussing the day's occurrences. Other familiar foods, like traditional roast chicken, fish pie and baked potatoes, are all covered in this chapter so, whenever you need them, you'll have heartening recipes to hand, just like the ones your Grandma might have cooked for you.*

# TOMATO SOUP

**SERVES 4**
55 g/2 oz butter
I onion, finely chopped
700 g/I lb 9 oz tomatoes, finely chopped
salt and pepper
600 ml/I pint hot chicken or
    vegetable stock

pinch of sugar
2 tbsp shredded fresh basil leaves, plus
    extra sprigs to garnish
I tbsp chopped fresh parsley
croûtons, to serve (optional)

**GRANDMA'S TIPS**

*When fresh tomatoes are out of season and tasteless, use 800 g/ 1 lb 12 oz canned tomatoes. Using canned tomatoes will not only give your soup some extra sweetness, but will also save you time. For a special treat and for extra warmth in the winter, add a tablespoon of sherry to each bowl before serving.*

**1** Melt half the butter in a large, heavy-based saucepan. Add the onion and cook over a low heat, stirring occasionally, for 5 minutes, or until softened. Add the tomatoes, season to taste with salt and pepper and cook for 5 minutes.

**2** Pour in the hot chicken or vegetable stock, return to the boil, then reduce the heat and cook for 10 minutes.

**3** Push the soup through a sieve with the back of a wooden spoon to remove the tomato skins and seeds. Return to the saucepan and stir in the sugar, remaining butter, basil and parsley. Heat through briefly, but do not allow to boil. Ladle into warmed serving bowls. Serve immediately, garnished with sprigs of basil and accompanied by croûtons, if you wish.

# CREAM OF CHICKEN SOUP

**SERVES 4**
3 tbsp butter
4 shallots, chopped
1 leek, trimmed and sliced
450 g/1 lb skinless chicken breasts, chopped
600 ml/1 pint chicken stock

1 tbsp chopped fresh parsley
1 tbsp chopped fresh thyme
salt and pepper
175 ml/6 fl oz double cream
sprigs of fresh thyme, to garnish
fresh crusty rolls, to serve

*GRANDMA'S TIPS*

*If you have just cooked a whole chicken for a meal, you can make a stock with the leftovers. Place the carcass in a large saucepan of water along with a chopped onion, carrot and celery stick. Bring to the boil, then simmer for 1–1¼ hours. Strain and carefully remove any meat from the bones and set aside. Make the soup according to the recipe, adding the cooked chicken pieces either before blending or just before serving.*

1 Melt the butter in a large saucepan over a medium heat. Add the shallots and cook, stirring, for 3 minutes, until slightly softened. Add the leek and cook for a further 5 minutes, stirring. Add the chicken, stock and herbs, and season with salt and pepper. Bring to the boil, then lower the heat and simmer for 25 minutes, until the chicken is tender and cooked through. Remove from the heat and leave to cool for 10 minutes.

2 Transfer the soup into a food processor and blend until smooth (you may need to do this in batches). Return the soup to the pan and warm over a low heat for 5 minutes.

3 Stir in the cream and cook for a further 2 minutes, then remove from the heat and ladle into serving bowls. Garnish with sprigs of thyme and serve with fresh crusty rolls.

# GRILLED CHEESE SANDWICH

**SERVES 2**

100 g/3½ oz Gruyère or Emmental
  cheese, grated
4 slices white bread, with the crusts
  trimmed
2 thick slices ham
1 small egg, beaten
3 tbsp unsalted butter, plus extra if
  necessary

**for the white sauce**

2 tbsp unsalted butter
1 tsp sunflower oil
½ tbsp plain flour
125 ml/4 fl oz warm milk
pepper

**1** Spread half the cheese on 2 bread slices, then top each with a slice of ham, cut to fit. Sprinkle the ham with all but 2 tablespoons of the remaining cheese, then sandwich together with the remaining bread slices and press down well.

**2** To make the sauce, melt the butter with the oil in a small, heavy-based pan and stir in the flour until well combined and smooth. Cook over a medium heat, stirring constantly, for 1 minute. Remove from the heat and stir in a little of the milk until well incorporated. Return to the heat and gradually add the remaining milk, stirring constantly, until it has all been incorporated. Cook for a further 3 minutes, or until the sauce is smooth and thickened. Stir in the remaining cheese and pepper to taste, then set aside and keep warm.

**3** Beat the egg in a shallow dish. Add 1 sandwich and press down to coat on both sides, then remove from the dish and repeat with the other sandwich.

**4** Preheat the grill to high. Line a baking tray with foil and set aside. Melt the butter in a sauté pan or frying pan and cook 1 or both sandwiches, depending on the size of your pan, over a medium-high heat until golden brown on both sides. Add a little extra butter, if necessary, if you have to cook the sandwiches separately.

**5** Transfer the sandwiches to the foil-lined baking tray and spread the white sauce over the top. Cook under the grill, about 10 cm/4 inches from the heat, for 4 minutes, or until golden and brown.

# BACON BUTTIES

**SERVES I**
2 smoked bacon rashers
15 g/½ oz butter, softened
2 slices thick white or brown bread

pepper
1 tomato, sliced (optional)
sauce of choice (brown sauce, tomato
  ketchup or mustard)

**GRANDMA'S TIPS**

*These traditional 'door-step' butties can be made using thinly sliced bread with the addition of lettuce to make a BLT (bacon, lettuce and tomato) – the sauce is optional. For an even more exotic sarnie, add some slices of avocado.*

**1** Cut the rashers of bacon in half so that you have 2 pieces of back bacon and 2 pieces of streaky.

**2** Place the bacon under a hot grill and grill, turning frequently, until the bacon is cooked and as crispy as you like it.

**3** Meanwhile, butter the bread.

**4** Place 2 pieces of bacon on one slice of bread and season with a grinding of pepper. Add the tomato, if using, and the sauce. Top with the remaining bacon and the other slice of bread and eat immediately.

# ROAST CHICKEN

**SERVES 6**

1 free-range chicken, weighing 2.25 kg/
  5 lb
55 g/2 oz butter
2 tbsp chopped fresh lemon thyme

salt and pepper
1 lemon, quartered
125 ml/4 fl oz white wine
6 fresh thyme sprigs, to garnish

**GRANDMA'S TIPS**

*This is the quintessential roast chicken recipe. If you want even more flavour to the bird, stuff it with a finely chopped onion, the grated rind and juice of 1 lemon and some fresh thyme leaves mixed with a few soft breadcrumbs. For an even more robust variation, stuff the bird with 40 cloves of garlic – it will be delicious and milder than you might think, as the cooking renders the garlic sweet and not so pungent.*

1  Preheat the oven to 220°C/425°F/Gas Mark 7. Make sure the chicken is clean, wiping it inside and out using kitchen paper, and place in a roasting tin.

2  Place the butter in a bowl and soften with a fork, then mix in the thyme and season well with salt and pepper. Butter the chicken all over with the herb butter, inside and out, and place the lemon quarters inside the body cavity. Pour the wine over the chicken.

3  Roast the chicken in the centre of the oven for 20 minutes. Reduce the temperature to 190°C/375°F/Gas Mark 5 and continue to roast for a further 1¼ hours, basting frequently. Cover with foil if the skin begins to brown too much. If the tin dries out, add a little more wine or water.

4  Test that the chicken is cooked by piercing the thickest part of the leg with a sharp knife or skewer and making sure the juices run clear. Remove from the oven.

5  Remove the chicken from the roasting tin and place on a warmed serving plate to rest, covered with foil, for 10 minutes before carving.

6  Place the roasting tin on the top of the hob and bubble the pan juices gently over a low heat until they have reduced and are thick and glossy. Season to taste with salt and pepper.

7  Serve the chicken with the pan juices and scatter with the thyme sprigs.

# POTATO, LEEK & CHICKEN PIE

**SERVES 4**

225 g/8 oz waxy potatoes, cubed
5 tbsp butter
I skinless chicken breast fillet, about
   175 g/6 oz, cubed
I leek, sliced
150 g/5½ oz chestnut mushrooms, sliced

2½ tbsp plain flour
300 ml/10 fl oz milk
I tbsp Dijon mustard
2 tbsp chopped fresh sage
225 g/8 oz filo pastry, thawed if frozen
3 tbsp butter, melted
salt and pepper

**1** Preheat the oven to 180°C/350°F/Gas Mark 4. Cook the potato cubes in a saucepan of boiling water for 5 minutes. Drain and set aside.

**2** Melt the butter in a frying pan and cook the chicken cubes for 5 minutes or until browned all over.

**3** Add the leek and mushrooms and cook for 3 minutes, stirring. Stir in the flour and cook for 1 minute stirring constantly. Gradually stir in the milk and bring to the boil. Add the mustard, sage and potato cubes, season to taste with salt and pepper and simmer for 10 minutes.

**4** Meanwhile, line a deep pie dish with half of the sheets of filo pastry. Spoon the sauce into the dish and cover with 1 sheet of pastry. Brush the pastry with butter and lay another sheet on top. Brush this sheet with butter.

**5** Cut the remaining filo pastry into strips and fold them on to the top of the pie to create a ruffled effect. Brush the strips with the melted butter and cook in the preheated oven for 45 minutes or until golden brown and crisp. Serve hot.

# ROAST BEEF

**SERVES 8**

1 prime rib of beef joint, weighing
   2.7 kg/6 lb
salt and pepper
2 tsp dry English mustard

3 tbsp plain flour
300 ml/10 fl oz red wine
300 ml/10 fl oz beef stock
2 tsp Worcestershire sauce (optional)
Yorkshire pudding, to serve

**GRANDMA'S TIPS**

*Instead of making a traditional gravy, you can just pour off the fat and add enough red wine to deglaze the pan. Season to taste and serve immediately. This is known as a 'jus'.*

1 Preheat the oven to 230°C/450°F/Gas Mark 8.

2 Season the meat to taste with salt and pepper. Rub in the mustard and 1 tablespoon of the flour.

3 Place the meat in a roasting tin large enough to hold it comfortably and roast in the oven for 15 minutes. Reduce the temperature to 190°C/375°F/Gas Mark 5 and cook for 15 minutes per 450 g/1 lb, plus 15 minutes (1¾ hours for this joint) for rare beef or 20 minutes per 450 g/1 lb, plus 20 minutes (2 hours 20 minutes) for medium beef. Baste the meat from time to time to keep it moist, and if the tin becomes too dry, add a little stock or red wine.

4 Remove the meat from the oven and place on a warmed serving plate, cover with foil and leave in a warm place for 10–15 minutes.

5 To make the gravy, pour off most of the fat from the tin, leaving behind the meat juices and the sediment. Place the tin on the hob over a medium heat and scrape all the sediment from the base of the tin. Sprinkle in the remaining flour and quickly mix it into the juices with a small whisk. When you have a smooth paste, gradually add the wine and most of the stock, whisking constantly. Bring to the boil, then reduce the heat to a gentle simmer and cook for 2–3 minutes. Season to taste with salt and pepper and add the remaining stock, if needed, and a little Worcestershire sauce, if you like.

6 When ready to serve, carve the meat into slices and serve on warmed plates. Pour the gravy into a warmed jug and take direct to the table. Serve with Yorkshire pudding.

# BEEF STEW WITH HERB DUMPLINGS

**SERVES 6**
3 tbsp olive oil
2 onions, finely sliced
2 garlic cloves, chopped
1 kg/2 lb 4 oz good-quality braising steak
2 tbsp plain flour
salt and pepper
300 ml/10 fl oz beef stock
bouquet garni
150 ml/5 fl oz red wine
1 tbsp chopped fresh parsley, to garnish

**for the herb dumplings**
115 g/4 oz self-raising flour, plus extra
  for shaping
55 g/2 oz suet or vegetable shortening
1 tsp mustard
1 tbsp chopped fresh parsley
1 tsp chopped fresh sage
salt and pepper
4 tbsp cold water

## GRANDMA'S TIPS

*You can make the stew the day before and refrigerate it overnight. Reheat 20 minutes before you're ready to add the dumplings, and proceed with the recipe. This will enhance the flavour of the stew and makes for fresh and light dumplings. You can vary the herbs used — try rosemary or thyme — and add some crushed garlic if you like.*

**1** Preheat the oven to 150°C/300°F/Gas Mark 2.

**2** Heat 1 tablespoon of the oil in a large frying pan and fry the onion and garlic until soft and brown. Remove from the pan using a slotted spoon and place in a large casserole dish.

**3** Trim the meat and cut into thick strips. Using the remaining oil, fry the meat in the frying pan over a high heat, stirring well until it is brown all over.

**4** Sprinkle in the flour and stir well to prevent lumps. Season well with salt and pepper.

**5** Over a medium heat, pour in the stock, stirring all the time to make a smooth sauce, then continue to heat until boiling.

**6** Carefully turn the contents of the frying pan into the casserole dish. Add the bouquet garni and the wine. Cover and cook gently for 2–2½ hours.

**7** Start making the dumplings 20 minutes before the stew is ready. Place the flour, suet, mustard, parsley, sage, and salt and pepper to taste in a bowl and mix well. Just before adding the dumplings to the stew, add enough of the water to the mixture to form a firm but soft dough. Break the dough into 12 pieces and roll them into round dumplings (you might need some flour on your hands for this).

**8** Remove the stew from the oven, check the seasoning, discard the bouquet garni and add the dumplings, pushing them down under the liquid. Cover and return the dish to the oven, continuing to cook for 15 minutes until the dumplings have doubled in size.

**9** Serve piping hot with the parsley scattered over the top.

# STEAK & KIDNEY PIE

**SERVES 4–6**

butter, for greasing
700 g/1 lb 9 oz braising steak, trimmed
   and cut into 4-cm/1½-inch pieces
3 lambs' kidneys, cored and cut into
   2.5-cm/1-inch pieces
2 tbsp plain flour, plus extra for dusting
salt and pepper

3 tbsp vegetable oil
1 onion, roughly chopped
1 garlic clove, finely chopped
125 ml/4 fl oz red wine
450 ml/16 fl oz stock
1 bay leaf
400 g/14 oz ready-made puff pastry
1 egg, beaten

**1** Preheat the oven to 160°C/325°F/Gas Mark 3. Grease a 1.2-litre/2-pint pie dish.

**2** Put the prepared meat with the flour and salt and pepper in a large plastic bag and shake until all the meat is well coated.

**3** Heat the oil in a flameproof casserole over a high heat and brown the meat in batches. Remove from the casserole with a slotted spoon and keep warm. Fry the onion and garlic in the casserole for 2–3 minutes until softening.

**4** Stir in the wine and scrape the base of the pan to release the sediment. Pour in the stock, stirring constantly, and bring to the boil. Bubble for 2–3 minutes. Add the bay leaf and return the meat to the casserole. Cover and cook in the centre of the oven for 1½–2 hours. Check the seasoning, then remove the bay leaf. Leave the meat to cool, preferably overnight, to develop the flavours.

**5** Preheat the oven to 200°C/400°F/Gas Mark 6.

**6** Roll out the pastry on a lightly floured work surface to about 7 cm/2¾ inches larger than the pie dish. Cut off a 3-cm/1¼-inch strip from the edge. Moisten the rim of the dish and press the pastry strip onto it. Place the pie funnel in the centre of the dish and spoon in the steak and kidney filling. Don't overfill, keeping any extra gravy to serve separately. Moisten the pastry collar with water and put on the pastry lid, taking care to fit it carefully around the pie funnel. Crimp the edges of the pastry firmly and glaze with the egg.

**7** Place the pie on a tray towards the top of the oven for about 30 minutes. The pie should be golden brown and the filling bubbling hot; cover it with foil and reduce the temperature if the pastry is getting too brown.

# HAMBURGERS

**SERVES 4–6**
450 g/1 lb rump steak or topside,
   freshly minced
1 onion, grated
2–4 garlic cloves, crushed
2 tsp wholegrain mustard
pepper
2 tbsp olive oil

450 g/1 lb onions, finely sliced
2 tsp light muscovado sugar

**to serve**
4–6 sesame seed buns
lettuce
ketchup (optional)

**GRANDMA'S TIPS**
*Make a large batch and freeze,
individually wrapped or stored in
a plastic container with baking
parchment between the burgers to
keep them separate.*

1  Place the minced steak, grated onion, garlic, mustard and pepper in a large bowl and mix together. Shape into 4–6 equal-sized burgers, then cover and leave to chill for 30 minutes.

2  Meanwhile, heat the oil in a heavy-based frying pan. Add the onions and cook over a low heat for 10–15 minutes, or until the onions have caramelized. Add the sugar after 8 minutes and stir occasionally during cooking. Drain well on kitchen paper and keep warm.

3  Wipe the frying pan clean, then heat until hot. When hot, add the burgers and cook for 3–5 minutes on each side or until cooked to personal preference. Serve in sesame seed buns with the onions, lettuce and ketchup, if you like.

# SHEPHERD'S PIE

**SERVES 6**
1 tbsp olive oil
2 onions, finely chopped
2 garlic cloves, finely chopped
675 g/1 lb 8 oz good-quality lamb mince
2 carrots, finely chopped
salt and pepper
1 tbsp plain flour
225 ml/8 fl oz beef or chicken stock
125 ml/4 fl oz red wine
Worcestershire sauce (optional)

**for the mashed potato**
675g g/1 lb 8 oz floury potatoes, such as
    King Edwards, Maris Piper or Desirée,
    peeled and cut into even-sized chunks
55 g/2 oz butter
2 tbsp cream or milk
salt and pepper

**GRANDMA'S TIPS**

*To make a cottage pie, use minced beef instead of the lamb. Instead of the basic mashed potato topping, you could try using a mixture of mashed potatoes and carrot or parsnip. Alternatively, substitute grated potato for the mashed potatoes for a 'rösti-style' topping.*

**1** Preheat the oven to 180°C/350°F/Gas Mark 4.

**2** Heat the oil in a large, flameproof casserole dish and fry the onion until softened, then add the garlic and stir well.

**3** Raise the heat and add the meat. Cook quickly to brown the meat all over, stirring continually. Add the carrots and season well with salt and pepper.

**4** Stir in the flour and add the stock and wine. Stir well and heat until simmering and thickened.

**5** Cover the casserole dish and cook in the oven for about 1 hour. Check the consistency from time to time and add a little more stock or wine if required. The meat mixture should be quite thick but not dry. Season with salt and pepper to taste and add a little Worcestershire sauce, if desired.

**6** While the meat is cooking, make the mashed potato. Cook the potatoes in a large saucepan of boiling salted water for 15–20 minutes. Drain well and mash with a potato masher until smooth. Add the butter and cream and season well with salt and pepper.

**7** Spoon the lamb mixture into an ovenproof serving dish and spread or pipe the potato on top.

**8** Increase the oven temperature to 200°C/400°F/Gas Mark 6 and cook the pie for 15–20 minutes at the top of the oven until golden brown. You might like to finish it off under a medium grill for a really crisp brown topping to the potato.

# LAMB SHANKS WITH CANNELLINI BEANS

**SERVES 4**

250 g/9 oz cannellini beans, soaked
  overnight
2 tbsp sunflower oil
1 large onion, thinly sliced
4 carrots, chopped
2 celery sticks, thinly sliced
1 garlic clove, chopped

4 large lamb shanks
400 g/14 oz canned chopped tomatoes
300 ml/10 fl oz red wine
finely pared zest and juice of 1 orange
2 bay leaves
3 rosemary sprigs
225 ml/8 fl oz water
salt and pepper

**1** Preheat the oven to 160°C/325°F/Gas Mark 3. Drain the soaked beans and rinse under cold running water. Put in a large pan of cold water, bring to the boil and skim off any scum, then boil rapidly for 10 minutes. Drain and set aside.

**2** Meanwhile, heat the oil in a large, flameproof casserole, add the onion, and cook for 5 minutes, or until softened. Add the carrots and celery and cook for a further 5 minutes, or until beginning to soften and the onion is beginning to brown. Add the garlic and cook for a further 1 minute. Push the vegetables to the sides of the pan.

**3** Add the lamb shanks to the pan and cook for about 5 minutes, until browned on all sides. Add the beans to the pan with the tomatoes, wine and orange zest and juice, and stir together. Add the bay leaves and rosemary. Pour in the water so that the liquid comes halfway up the shanks. Season with pepper but do not add salt as this will stop the beans from softening.

**4** Bring to the boil, then cover the pan and cook in the oven for about 1 hour. Turn the shanks over in the stock then continue cooking for 1½ hours until the lamb and beans are tender. Remove the bay leaves, then taste and add salt and pepper if necessary. Serve hot.

# TOAD IN THE HOLE

**SERVES 4**
oil, for greasing
115 g/4 oz plain flour
pinch of salt

1 egg, beaten
300 ml/10 fl oz milk
450 g/1 lb good-quality pork sausages
1 tbsp vegetable oil

**GRANDMA'S TIPS**
*Try making toad in the hole with meat balls instead of sausages. Fried onion rings can also be added to the dish before adding the batter.*

1  Grease a 20 x 25-cm/8 x 10-inch ovenproof dish or roasting tin.

2  Make the batter by sifting the flour and salt into a mixing bowl. Make a well in the centre and add the beaten egg and half the milk. Carefully stir the liquid into the flour until the mixture is smooth. Gradually beat in the remaining milk. Leave to stand for 30 minutes.

3  Preheat the oven to 220°C/425°F/Gas Mark 7.

4  Prick the sausages and place them in the dish. Sprinkle over the oil and cook the sausages in the oven for 10 minutes until they are beginning to colour and the fat has started to run and is sizzling.

5  Remove from the oven and quickly pour the batter over the sausages. Return to the oven and cook for 35–45 minutes until the batter is well risen and golden brown. Serve immediately.

# FISH & CHIPS

**SERVES 2**
vegetable oil, for deep-frying
3 large potatoes, such as Cara or Desirée
2 thick cod or haddock fillets,
    175 g/6 oz each

salt and pepper
175 g/6 oz self-raising flour, plus extra
    for dusting
200 ml/7 fl oz cold lager
lemon wedges, to serve

1 Heat the oil in a temperature-controlled deep-fat fryer to 120°C/250°F, or in a heavy-based saucepan, checking the temperature with a thermometer, to blanch the chips. Preheat the oven to 150°C/300°F/Gas Mark 2.

2 Peel the potatoes and cut into even-sized chips. Fry for about 8–10 minutes, depending on size, until softened but not coloured. Remove from the oil, drain on kitchen paper and place in a warm dish in the warm oven. Increase the temperature of the oil to 180–190°C/350–375°F, or until a cube of bread browns in 30 seconds.

3 Meanwhile, season the fish with salt and pepper and dust it lightly with a little flour.

4 Make a thick batter by sieving the flour into a bowl with a little salt and whisking in most of the lager. Check the consistency before adding the remainder: it should be very thick, like double cream.

5 Dip one fillet into the batter and allow it to be thickly coated. Carefully place the fish in the hot oil, then repeat with the other fillet.

6 Cook for 8–10 minutes, depending on the thickness of the fish. Turn the fillets over halfway through the cooking time. Remove the fish from the fryer or saucepan, drain and keep warm.

7 Make sure the oil temperature is still at 180°C/350°F and return the chips to the fryer or saucepan. Cook for a further 2–3 minutes until golden brown and crispy. Drain and season with salt and pepper before serving with the battered fish and lemon wedges for squeezing over.

# FISHERMAN'S PIE

**SERVES 6**

butter, for greasing
900 g/2 lb white fish fillets, such as
    plaice, skinned
salt and pepper
150 ml/5 fl oz dry white wine
1 tbsp chopped fresh parsley, tarragon
    or dill

175 g/6 oz small mushrooms, sliced
100 g/3½ oz butter
175 g/6 oz cooked peeled prawns
40 g/1½ oz plain flour
125 ml/4 fl oz double cream
900 g/2 lb floury potatoes, such as King
    Edwards, Maris Piper or Desirée,
    peeled and cut into even-sized chunks

**1** Preheat the oven to 180°C/350°F/Gas Mark 4. Butter a 1.7-litre/3-pint baking dish.

**2** Fold the fish fillets in half and place in the dish. Season well with salt and pepper, pour over the wine and scatter over the herbs.

**3** Cover with foil and bake for 15 minutes until the fish starts to flake. Strain off the liquid and reserve for the sauce. Increase the oven temperature to 220°C/425°F/Gas Mark 7.

**4** Sauté the mushrooms in a frying pan with 15 g/½ oz of the butter and spoon over the fish. Scatter over the prawns.

**5** Heat 55 g/2 oz of the butter in a saucepan and stir in the flour. Cook for a few minutes without browning, remove from the heat, then add the reserved cooking liquid gradually, stirring well between each addition.

**6** Return to the heat and gently bring to the boil, still stirring to ensure a smooth sauce. Add the cream and season to taste with salt and pepper. Pour over the fish in the dish and smooth over the surface.

**7** Make the mashed potato by cooking the potatoes in boiling salted water for 15–20 minutes. Drain well and mash with a potato masher until smooth. Season to taste with salt and pepper and add the remaining butter, stirring until melted.

**8** Pile or pipe the potato onto the fish and sauce and bake for 10–15 minutes until golden brown.

# SALMON FISHCAKES

**SERVES 4**
700 g/1 lb 9 oz skinless salmon fillet, cut into cubes
300 ml/10 fl oz full-fat milk
1 bay leaf
100 g/3½ oz broccoli, steamed until tender
700 g/1 lb 9 oz potatoes, boiled and mashed

2 tbsp finely chopped fresh parsley
4 tbsp wholemeal plain flour
pepper
1 egg yolk
2 large eggs, beaten
150 g/5½ oz fresh wholemeal breadcrumbs
2 tbsp olive oil

## GRANDMA'S TIPS

*These absolutely delicious fishcakes can be made more economical by using canned salmon. The broccoli can be replaced with sautéed leeks or even some sweetcorn, which the kids will love. For a more sophisticated flavour, chopped dill can be used instead of the parsley and the fishcakes can be served with a dill sauce or mayonnaise.*

1 Preheat the oven to 200°C/400°F/Gas Mark 6. Put the salmon in a saucepan with the milk and bay leaf and bring slowly up to a simmer. Simmer for 2 minutes, then remove the saucepan from the heat, lift out and discard the bay leaf and leave the fish in the milk to cool. When cooled, lift out the fish with a slotted spoon onto kitchen paper to drain.

2 Flake the fish into a large bowl. Put the broccoli in a food processor and pulse until smooth. Add to the fish with the mashed potatoes, parsley, 1 tablespoon of the flour, and pepper to taste. Add the egg yolk and mix well. If the mixture is a little dry, add some of the poaching milk; if too wet, add a little more flour.

3 Divide the mixture into 12 portions and shape each portion into a cake. Put the beaten eggs, remaining flour and the breadcrumbs on 3 separate plates. Roll each fishcake in the flour, then in the beaten egg, and then in the breadcrumbs to coat.

4 Heat the oil in a non-stick baking tray in the preheated oven for 5 minutes. Add the fishcakes and bake for 10 minutes, then carefully turn the fishcakes over and bake for a further 10 minutes. Serve hot.

# WINTER VEGETABLE COBBLER

**SERVES 4**
1 tbsp olive oil
1 garlic clove, crushed
8 small onions, halved
2 celery sticks, sliced
225 g/8 oz swede, chopped
2 carrots, sliced
½ small head of cauliflower, broken into
  florets
225 g/8 oz button mushrooms, sliced
400 g/14 oz canned chopped tomatoes
55 g/2 oz red lentils, rinsed
2 tbsp cornflour
3–4 tbsp water

300 ml/10 fl oz vegetable stock
2 tsp Tabasco sauce
2 tsp chopped fresh oregano
fresh oregano sprigs, to garnish

**for the topping**
225 g/8 oz self-raising flour
pinch of salt
4 tbsp butter
115 g/4 oz grated mature Cheddar
  cheese
2 tsp chopped fresh oregano
1 egg, lightly beaten
150 ml/5 fl oz milk

**GRANDMA'S TIPS**

*This rib-sticking dish is just the thing for those cold winter evenings. The vegetables can be varied according to taste and season. You might like to make a curry-flavoured cobbler by using curry paste instead of the Tabasco sauce. The topping can be made with wholemeal flour instead of white for a healthier version.*

1  Preheat the oven to 180°C/350°F/Gas Mark 4. Heat the oil in a large frying pan and cook the garlic and onions over a low heat for 5 minutes. Add the celery, swede, carrots and cauliflower and cook for 2–3 minutes.

2  Add the mushrooms, tomatoes and lentils. Place the cornflour and water in a bowl and mix to make a smooth paste. Stir into the frying pan with the stock, Tabasco and oregano. Transfer to an ovenproof dish, cover and bake in the preheated oven for 20 minutes.

3  To make the topping, sift the flour and salt into a bowl. Add the butter and rub it in, then stir in most of the cheese and oregano. Beat the egg with the milk in a small bowl and add enough to the dry ingredients to make a soft dough. Knead, then roll out on a lightly floured work surface to 1 cm/½ inch thick. Cut into 5-cm/2-inch rounds.

4  Remove the dish from the oven and increase the temperature to 200°C/400°F/Gas Mark 6. Arrange the dough rounds around the edge of the dish, brush with the remaining egg and milk mixture and sprinkle with the reserved cheese. Cook for a further 10–12 minutes. Garnish with oregano sprigs and serve.

# ROASTED BUTTERNUT SQUASH RISOTTO

**SERVES 4**

600 g/1 lb 5 oz butternut squash or
  pumpkin, peeled and cut into
  bite-sized pieces
4 tbsp olive oil
1 tsp clear honey
25 g/1 oz fresh basil, plus extra sprigs
  to garnish

25 g/1 oz fresh oregano
1 tbsp margarine
2 onions, finely chopped
450 g/1 lb arborio or other risotto rice
175 ml/6 fl oz dry white wine
1.2 litres/2 pints vegetable stock
salt and pepper

**1** Preheat the oven to 200°C/400°F/Gas Mark 6. Put the squash into a roasting tin. Mix 1 tablespoon of the oil with the honey and spoon over the squash. Turn the squash to coat it in the mixture. Roast in the preheated oven for 30–35 minutes, or until tender.

**2** Meanwhile, put the basil and oregano into a food processor with 2 tablespoons of the remaining oil and process until finely chopped and blended. Set aside.

**3** Heat the margarine and remaining oil in a large, heavy-based saucepan over a medium heat. Add the onions and fry, stirring occasionally, for 8 minutes, or until soft and golden. Add the rice and cook for 2 minutes, stirring to coat the grains in the oil mixture.

**4** Pour in the wine and bring to the boil. Reduce the heat slightly and cook until the wine is almost absorbed. Add the stock, a little at a time, and cook over a medium-low heat, stirring constantly, for 20 minutes.

**5** Gently stir in the herb oil and squash until thoroughly mixed into the rice and cook for a further 5 minutes, or until the rice is creamy and cooked but retaining a little bite in the centre of the grain. Season well with salt and pepper before serving, garnished with sprigs of basil.

# MACARONI CHEESE

**SERVES 4**
600 ml/1 pint milk
1 onion, peeled
8 peppercorns
1 bay leaf
55 g/2 oz butter
40 g/1½ oz plain flour
½ tsp ground nutmeg

5 tbsp double cream
pepper
100 g/3½ oz mature Cheddar cheese,
  grated
100 g/3½ oz Roquefort cheese, crumbled
350 g/12 oz dried macaroni
100 g/3½ oz Gruyère or Emmental
  cheese, grated

**GRANDMA'S TIPS**

*Macaroni cheese is a great family favourite. This rich version using three varieties of cheese can be made simpler by using one cheese, such as Cheddar, and omitting the cream. You can also add some vegetables – steamed broccoli florets or baby spinach leaves will add colour and extra vitamins.*

1  Put the milk, onion, peppercorns and bay leaf in a pan and bring to the boil. Remove from the heat and let stand for 15 minutes.

2  Melt the butter in a pan and stir in the flour until well combined and smooth. Cook over a medium heat, stirring constantly, for 1 minute. Remove from the heat. Strain the milk to remove the solids and stir a little into the butter and flour mixture until well incorporated. Return to the heat and gradually add the remaining milk, stirring constantly, until it has all been incorporated. Cook for a further 3 minutes, or until the sauce is smooth and thickened, then add the nutmeg, cream and pepper to taste. Add the Cheddar and Roquefort cheeses and stir until melted.

3  Meanwhile, bring a large pan of water to the boil. Add the macaroni, then return to the boil and cook for 8–10 minutes, or until just tender. Drain well and add to the cheese sauce. Stir well together.

4  Preheat the grill to high. Spoon the mixture into an ovenproof serving dish, then scatter over the Gruyère cheese and cook under the grill until bubbling and brown.

# SOUFFLÉD BAKED
POTATOES

**SERVES 4**

2 baking potatoes, scrubbed
1 tbsp olive oil
2 tbsp full-fat milk
25 g/1 oz butter
25 g/1 oz Cheddar or Gruyère cheese,
   grated

1 large egg, separated
salt and pepper
2 slices ham, cooked turkey or unsmoked
   bacon, chopped
2 tbsp finely grated Parmesan cheese
salad, to serve

**GRANDMA'S TIPS**

*Baked potatoes make for the perfect meal, particularly when they are stuffed with lots of tasty ingredients such as Bolognese or chilli sauce, flaked fish or ratatouille. Make sure the potatoes are baked through so that they're soft inside and the skins are firm and crispy, which makes them most delicious.*
*You can even rub salt into the skins with the oil to enhance the flavour.*

1  Preheat the oven to 200°C/400°F/Gas Mark 6. Prick the potatoes with a fork. Rub the oil all over the potatoes, place on a baking sheet and bake in the preheated oven for 1 hour, or until the flesh is soft.

2  Remove the potatoes from the oven, cut in half lengthways and carefully scoop out the flesh into a bowl, keeping the skins intact. Set the skins aside.

3  Add the milk, butter, Cheddar cheese and egg yolk to the potato and mash well. Season to taste with salt and pepper. Mix in the ham.

4  In a separate, grease-free bowl, whisk the egg white until stiff, then fold into the potato mixture.

5  Pile the potato mixture back into the skins and sprinkle over the Parmesan cheese. Return to the oven and bake for 20 minutes. Serve with salad.

# SPAGHETTI WITH MEATBALLS

**SERVES 6**
1 potato, diced
salt and pepper
400 g/14 oz fresh beef mince
1 onion, finely chopped
1 egg
4 tbsp chopped fresh flat-leaf parsley
plain flour, for dusting

5 tbsp olive oil
400 ml/14 fl oz passata
2 tbsp tomato purée
450 g/1 lb dried spaghetti

**to garnish**
6 fresh basil leaves, shredded
Parmesan cheese shavings

**GRANDMA'S TIPS**

*Meatballs are a traditional accompaniment to spaghetti. They can be made with minced beef as here or with minced lamb or pork. A variety of ingredients can be added to give the dish a distinct taste – garlic can be used, as can herbs like oregano or marjoram. If time is short, substitute fresh breadcrumbs for the potato.*

1  Place the potato in a small pan, add cold water to cover and a pinch of salt and bring to the boil. Cook for 10–15 minutes, until tender, then drain. Either mash thoroughly with a potato masher or fork or pass through a potato ricer.

2  Combine the potato, beef, onion, egg and parsley in a bowl and season to taste with salt and pepper. Spread out the flour on a plate. With dampened hands, shape the meat mixture into walnut-size balls and roll in the flour. Shake off any excess.

3  Heat the oil in a heavy-based frying pan, add the meatballs and cook over a medium heat, stirring and turning frequently, for 8–10 minutes, until golden all over.

4  Add the passata and tomato purée and cook for a further 10 minutes, until the sauce is reduced and thickened.

5  Meanwhile, bring a large saucepan of lightly salted water to the boil. Add the pasta, bring back to the boil and cook for 8–10 minutes, until tender, but still firm to the bite.

6  Drain well and add to the meatball sauce, tossing well to coat. Transfer to a warm serving dish, garnish with the basil leaves and Parmesan and serve immediately.

# FETTUCCINE ALFREDO

**SERVES 4**
2 tbsp butter
200 ml/7 fl oz double cream
salt and pepper
450 g/l lb fresh fettuccine

85 g/3 oz freshly grated Parmesan
   cheese, plus extra to serve
pinch of freshly grated nutmeg
fresh flat-leaf parsley sprigs, to garnish

**1** Put the butter and 150 ml/5 fl oz of the cream into a large pan and bring the mixture to the boil over a medium heat. Reduce the heat, then simmer gently for 1½ minutes, or until the cream has thickened slightly.

**2** Meanwhile, bring a large pan of lightly salted water to the boil over medium heat. Add the pasta and cook for 2–3 minutes, or until tender, but still firm to the bite. Drain thoroughly and return to the pan, then pour over the cream sauce.

**3** Toss the pasta in the sauce over a low heat, stirring with a wooden spoon, until coated thoroughly.

**4** Add the remaining cream, Parmesan cheese and nutmeg to the pasta mixture and season to taste with salt and pepper. Toss the pasta in the mixture while heating through.

**5** Transfer the pasta mixture to warmed serving bowls and garnish with fresh parsley sprigs. Serve immediately with extra grated Parmesan cheese.

# LASAGNE AL FORNO

**SERVES 4**
2 tbsp olive oil
55 g/2 oz pancetta or rindless streaky
  bacon, chopped
1 onion, chopped
1 garlic clove, finely chopped
225 g/8 oz fresh beef mince
2 celery sticks, chopped
2 carrots, chopped
salt and pepper
pinch of sugar
½ tsp dried oregano
400 g/14 oz canned chopped tomatoes
225 g/8 oz dried no-precook lasagne
  sheets
115 g/4 oz freshly grated Parmesan
  cheese, plus extra for sprinkling

**for the cheese sauce**
300 ml/10 fl oz milk
1 bay leaf
6 black peppercorns
slice of onion
blade of mace
2 tbsp butter
3 tbsp plain flour
2 tsp Dijon mustard
70 g/2½ oz Cheddar cheese, grated
70 g/2½ oz Gruyère cheese, grated
salt and pepper

**GRANDMA'S TIPS**

*This dish is quite complicated to make, as it requires you to make both a meat and a cheese sauce. To cheat a little, you can buy a ready-made cheese sauce to cut down on the preparation time. Make sure you use no-cook lasagne sheets as they will not need to be boiled before use.*

**1** Preheat the oven to 190°C/375°F/Gas Mark 5. Heat the olive oil in a large, heavy-based saucepan. Add the pancetta and cook over a medium heat, stirring occasionally, for 3 minutes, or until the fat begins to run. Add the onion and garlic and cook, stirring occasionally, for 5 minutes, or until softened.

**2** Add the beef and cook, breaking it up with a wooden spoon, until browned all over. Stir in the celery and carrots and cook for 5 minutes. Season to taste with salt and pepper. Add the sugar, oregano and tomatoes. Bring to the boil, reduce the heat and simmer for 30 minutes.

**3** Meanwhile, make the cheese sauce. Pour the milk into a saucepan and add the bay leaf, peppercorns, onion and mace. Heat gently to just below the boiling point, then remove from the heat, cover and leave to infuse for 10 minutes. Strain the milk into a jug. Melt the butter in a separate saucepan. Sprinkle in the flour and cook over a low heat, stirring constantly, for 1 minute. Remove from the heat and gradually stir in the warm milk. Return to the heat and bring to the boil, stirring. Cook, stirring, until thickened and smooth. Stir in the mustard and both cheeses, then season to taste with salt and pepper.

**4** In a large, rectangular ovenproof dish, make alternate layers of meat sauce, lasagne and Parmesan cheese. Pour the cheese sauce over the layers, covering them completely, and sprinkle with Parmesan cheese. Bake in the preheated oven for 30 minutes, or until golden brown and bubbling. Serve immediately.

# PIZZA MARGHERITA

**SERVES 4**
**for the pizza dough**
15 g/½ oz easy-blend dried yeast
I tsp sugar
250 ml/9 fl oz warm water
350 g/12 oz strong white flour, plus
   extra for dusting
I tsp salt
I tbsp olive oil, plus extra for oiling

**for the topping**
400 g/14 oz canned chopped tomatoes
2 garlic cloves, crushed
2 tsp dried basil
I tbsp olive oil
salt and pepper
2 tbsp tomato purée
100 g/3½ oz mozzarella cheese, chopped
2 tbsp freshly grated Parmesan cheese

## GRANDMA'S TIPS
*Nowadays pizza is served with all sorts of toppings – lots of them quite bizarre. This is a basic recipe that can be adapted to personal choice. Olives, both black and green, anchovy fillets, sliced mushrooms and salami all work well and add lots of colour and texture. Family members can make their own individual pizzas using their favourite toppings. Ready-made pizza bases are widely available and can be used when time is short.*

**1** Place the yeast and sugar in a measuring jug and mix with 50 ml/2 fl oz of the water. Leave the yeast mixture in a warm place for 15 minutes or until frothy.

**2** Mix the flour with the salt and make a well in the centre. Add the oil, the yeast mixture and the remaining water. Using a wooden spoon, mix to form a smooth dough.

**3** Turn the dough out onto a floured surface and knead for 4–5 minutes or until smooth.

**4** Return the dough to the bowl, cover with an oiled sheet of clingfilm and leave to rise for 30 minutes or until doubled in size.

**5** Knead the dough for 2 minutes. Stretch the dough with your hands, then place it on an oiled baking tray or pizza stone, pushing out the edges until even. The dough should be no more than 6 mm/¼ inch thick because it will rise during cooking.

**6** Preheat the oven to 200°C/400°F/Gas Mark 6. To make the topping, place the tomatoes, garlic, dried basil, olive oil and salt and pepper to taste in a large frying pan and leave to simmer for 20 minutes or until the sauce has thickened. Stir in the tomato purée and leave to cool slightly.

**7** Spread the topping evenly over the pizza base. Top with the mozzarella and Parmesan cheeses and bake in the preheated oven for 20–25 minutes. Serve hot.

# PAELLA

**SERVES 4–6**

1.2 litres/2 pints fish stock or water
12 large raw prawns, in their shells
½ tsp saffron threads
2 tbsp hot water
100 g/3½ oz skinless, boneless chicken breast, cut into ½-inch/1-cm pieces
100 g/3½ oz pork fillet, cut into ½-inch/1-cm pieces
salt and pepper
3 tbsp olive oil
100 g/3½ oz Spanish chorizo sausage, casing removed, cut into ½-inch/1-cm slices

1 large red onion, chopped
2 garlic cloves, crushed
½ tsp cayenne pepper
½ tsp paprika
1 red pepper, deseeded and sliced
1 green pepper, deseeded and sliced
12 cherry tomatoes, halved
350 g/12 oz medium-grain paella rice
1 tbsp chopped fresh parsley
2 tsp chopped fresh tarragon

**1** Put the stock in a large pan and bring to a simmer. Add the prawns and cook for 2 minutes. Using a slotted spoon, transfer the prawns to a bowl and set aside. Let the stock simmer. Put the saffron threads and water in a small bowl or cup and let infuse for a few minutes.

**2** Season the chicken and pork to taste with salt and pepper. Heat the oil in a paella pan or wide, shallow frying pan and cook the chicken, pork and chorizo over medium heat, stirring, for 5 minutes, or until golden. Add the onion and cook, stirring, for 2–3 minutes, or until softened. Add the garlic, cayenne pepper, paprika and saffron and its soaking liquid and cook, stirring constantly, for 1 minute. Add the pepper slices and tomato halves and cook, stirring, for a further 2 minutes.

**3** Add the rice and herbs and cook, stirring constantly, for 1 minute, or until the rice is glossy and coated. Pour in all but 100 ml/3½ fl oz of the hot stock and bring to the boil. Reduce the heat and let simmer, uncovered, for 10 minutes. Do not stir during cooking, but shake the pan once or twice. Season to taste with salt and pepper, then shake the pan and cook for a further 10 minutes, or until the rice grains are plump and almost cooked. If the liquid is absorbed too quickly, pour in a little more hot stock, then shake the pan to spread the liquid through the paella. Do not stir it in. Add the prawns and shake the pan, but do not stir. Cook for a further 2 minutes.

**4** When all the liquid has been absorbed and you detect a faint toasty aroma coming from the rice, remove from the heat immediately to prevent burning. Cover the pan with a clean tea towel or foil and let stand for 5 minutes. Divide the paella among warmed serving plates and serve immediately.

# COQ AU VIN

**SERVES 4**
4 tbsp butter
2 tbsp olive oil
1.8 kg/4 lb chicken pieces
115 g/4 oz rindless smoked bacon,
  cut into strips
115 g/4 oz baby onions
115 g/4 oz chestnut mushrooms, halved

2 garlic cloves, finely chopped
2 tbsp brandy
225 ml/8 fl oz red wine
300 ml/10 fl oz chicken stock
1 bouquet garni
salt and pepper
2 tbsp plain flour
bay leaves, to garnish

## GRANDMA'S TIPS

*Coq au vin is usually made with red wine, but it also can be made with white wine like a Riesling. If you're using white wine, add 125 ml/4 fl oz of single cream before serving and garnish with freshly chopped parsley.*

**1** Melt half the butter with the olive oil in a large, flameproof casserole. Add the chicken and cook over a medium heat, stirring, for 8–10 minutes, or until golden brown all over. Add the bacon, onions, mushrooms and garlic.

**2** Pour in the brandy and set it alight with a match or taper. When the flames have died down, add the wine, stock and bouquet garni and season to taste with salt and pepper. Bring to the boil, reduce the heat and simmer gently for 1 hour, or until the chicken pieces are cooked through and tender. Meanwhile, make a beurre manié by mashing the remaining butter with the flour in a small bowl.

**3** Remove and discard the bouquet garni. Transfer the chicken to a large plate and keep warm. Stir the beurre manié into the casserole, a little at a time. Bring to the boil, return the chicken to the casserole and serve immediately, garnished with bay leaves.

# BEEF BOURGUIGNON

**SERVES 4–6**

85 g/3 oz butter
2 tbsp sunflower oil
175 g/6 oz smoked lardons, blanched for
   30 seconds, drained and patted dry
900 g/2 lb braising beef, such as chuck
   or leg
2 large garlic cloves, crushed
1 carrot, diced
1 leek, halved and sliced
1 onion, finely chopped

2 tbsp plain flour
salt and pepper
350 ml/12 fl oz full-bodied red wine
about 500 ml/18 fl oz beef stock
1 tbsp tomato purée
1 bouquet garni
12 baby onions, peeled but kept whole
12 button mushrooms
chopped fresh flat-leaf parsley, to garnish
French bread, to serve

**1** Preheat the oven to 150°C/300°F/Gas Mark 2. Heat 25 g/1 oz of the butter and 1 tablespoon of the oil in a large, flameproof casserole. Cook the lardons over a medium-high heat, stirring, for 2 minutes, or until beginning to brown. Using a slotted spoon, remove from the casserole and drain on kitchen paper.

**2** Trim the beef and cut it into 5-cm/2-inch chunks. Add the beef to the casserole and cook over a high heat, stirring frequently, for 5 minutes, or until browned on all sides and sealed, adding more of the butter or oil to the casserole as necessary. Using a slotted spoon, transfer the beef to a plate.

**3** Pour off all but 2 tablespoons of the fat from the casserole. Add the garlic, carrot, leek and onion and cook over a medium heat, stirring frequently, for 3 minutes, or until the onion is beginning to soften. Sprinkle in the flour, season to taste with salt and pepper, and cook, stirring constantly, for 2 minutes, then remove from the heat.

**4** Gradually stir in the wine and stock and add the tomato purée and bouquet garni, then return to the heat and bring to the boil, stirring and scraping any sediment from the base of the casserole.

**5** Return the beef and lardons to the casserole and add extra stock if necessary so that the ingredients are covered by about 1 cm/½ inch of liquid. Slowly return to the boil, then cover and cook in the preheated oven for 2 hours.

**6** Meanwhile, heat 25 g/1 oz of the remaining butter and the remaining oil in a large sauté pan or frying pan and cook the baby onions over a medium-high heat, stirring frequently, until golden all over. Using a slotted spoon, transfer the onions to a plate.

**7** Heat the remaining butter in the pan and cook the mushrooms, stirring frequently, until golden brown. Remove from the pan and then stir them, with the onions, into the casserole, re-cover and cook for a further 30 minutes, or until the beef is very tender.

**8** Discard the bouquet garni, then adjust the seasoning to taste. Serve garnished with parsley, accompanied by plenty of French bread for mopping up all the juices.

# CHICKEN FAJITAS

**SERVES 4**

3 tbsp olive oil, plus extra for drizzling
3 tbsp maple syrup or clear honey
1 tbsp red wine vinegar
2 garlic cloves, crushed
2 tsp dried oregano

1–2 tsp dried red chilli flakes
salt and pepper
4 chicken breasts, skinless, boneless
2 red peppers, deseeded and cut into
    2.5-cm/1-inch strips
8 flour tortillas, warmed

**GRANDMA'S TIPS**

*Tortillas can be heated by wrapping in foil and placing in a warm oven for 3–4 minutes. Your family will enjoy wrapping their own fajitas – provide bowls of shredded lettuce, tomato salsa and soured cream to choose from.*

**1** Place the oil, maple syrup, vinegar, garlic, oregano, chilli flakes and salt and pepper to taste in a large, shallow dish or bowl and mix together.

**2** Slice the chicken across the grain into slices 2.5 cm/1 inch thick. Toss in the marinade until well coated. Cover and leave to chill in the refrigerator for 2–3 hours, turning occasionally.

**3** Heat a griddle pan until hot. Lift the chicken slices from the marinade with a slotted spoon, lay on the griddle pan and cook over medium-high heat for 3–4 minutes on each side, or until cooked through. Remove the chicken to a warmed serving plate and keep warm.

**4** Add the peppers, skin side down, to the griddle pan and cook for 2 minutes on each side. Transfer to the serving plate.

**5** Serve immediately with the warmed tortillas to be used as wraps.

# CHICKEN TIKKA MASALA

**SERVES 6**
½ onion, roughly chopped
55 g/2 oz tomato purée
1 tsp cumin seeds
2.5-cm/1-inch piece fresh root ginger, chopped
3 tbsp lemon juice
2 garlic cloves, crushed
2 tsp chilli powder
750 g/1 lb 10 oz boneless chicken
salt and pepper
fresh mint sprigs, to garnish

**for the masala sauce**
2 tbsp ghee
1 onion, sliced
1 tbsp black onion seeds
3 garlic cloves, crushed
2 fresh green chillies, chopped
200 g/7 oz canned chopped tomatoes
125 ml/4 fl oz low-fat natural yogurt
125 ml/4 fl oz coconut milk
1 tbsp chopped fresh coriander
1 tbsp chopped fresh mint
2 tbsp lemon or lime juice
½ tsp garam masala

**1** Combine the onion, tomato purée, cumin seeds, ginger, lemon juice, garlic and chilli powder in a food processor or blender and transfer to a bowl. Season to taste with salt and pepper. Cut chicken into 4-cm/1½-inch cubes. Stir into the bowl and leave for 2 hours.

**2** Make the masala sauce. Heat the ghee in a saucepan, add the onion and stir over a medium heat for 5 minutes. Add the black onion seeds, garlic and chillies. Add the tomatoes, yogurt and coconut milk, bring to the boil, then simmer for 20 minutes.

**3** Divide the chicken evenly between 8 oiled skewers and cook under a very hot preheated grill for 15 minutes, turning frequently. Remove the chicken and add to the sauce. Stir in the herbs, lemon juice and garam masala. Serve garnished with mint sprigs.

# VEGETABLE KORMA

**SERVES 4**
4 tbsp ghee or vegetable oil
2 onions, chopped
2 garlic cloves, chopped
1 fresh red chilli, chopped
1 tbsp grated fresh root ginger
2 tomatoes, peeled and chopped
1 orange pepper, deseeded and cut into
  small pieces
1 large potato, cut into chunks
200 g/7 oz cauliflower florets

½ tsp salt
1 tsp ground turmeric
1 tsp ground cumin
1 tsp ground coriander
1 tsp garam masala
200 ml/7 fl oz vegetable stock or water
150 ml/5 fl oz natural yogurt
150 ml/5 fl oz single cream
25 g/1 oz fresh coriander, chopped
freshly cooked rice, to serve

**GRANDMA'S TIPS**

*Try using other vegetables, such as green beans, okra, carrots and aubergines, to give a variety of flavours and textures. If you don't have all the spices just add 2 teaspoons of curry paste – or more if you are feeling brave!*

**1** Heat the ghee in a large saucepan over a medium heat, add the onions and garlic and cook, stirring, for 3 minutes. Add the chilli and ginger and cook for a further 4 minutes. Add the tomatoes, pepper, potato, cauliflower, salt and spices and cook, stirring, for a further 3 minutes. Stir in the stock and bring to the boil. Reduce the heat and simmer for 25 minutes.

**2** Stir in the yogurt and cream and cook, stirring, for a further 5 minutes. Add the fresh coriander and heat through.

**3** Serve the curry with freshly cooked rice.

# CHICKEN KIEV

**SERVES 4**
4 tbsp butter, softened
1 garlic clove, finely chopped
1 tbsp finely chopped fresh parsley
plus extra sprigs to garnish
1 tbsp finely chopped fresh oregano
salt and pepper
4 skinless, boneless chicken breasts
85 g/3 oz fresh white or wholemeal
breadcrumbs

3 tbsp freshly grated Parmesan cheese
1 egg, beaten
250 ml/9 fl oz vegetable oil, for
deep-frying

**to serve**
freshly cooked new potatoes
selection of cooked vegetables

1 Place the butter and garlic in a bowl and mix together well. Stir in the chopped herbs and season well with salt and pepper. Pound the chicken breasts to flatten them to an even thickness, then place a tablespoon of herb butter in the centre of each one. Fold in the sides to enclose the butter, then secure with cocktail sticks.

2 Combine the breadcrumbs and grated Parmesan on a plate. Dip the chicken parcels into the beaten egg, then coat in the breadcrumb mixture. Transfer to a plate, cover and chill for 30 minutes. Remove from the refrigerator and coat in the egg and then the breadcrumb mixture for a second time.

3 Pour the oil into a deep-fat fryer to a depth that will cover the chicken parcels. Heat until it reaches 180–190°C/350–375°F, or until a cube of bread browns in 30 seconds. Transfer the chicken to the hot oil and deep-fry for 5 minutes, or until cooked through. Lift out the chicken and drain on kitchen paper.

4 Divide the chicken among 4 serving plates, garnish with parsley sprigs and serve with new potatoes and a selection of vegetables.

# PORK CHOW MEIN

**SERVES 4**
250 g/9 oz egg noodles
4–5 tbsp vegetable oil
250 g/9 oz pork fillet, cooked
125g/4½ oz French beans
2 tbsp light soy sauce

1 tsp salt
½ tsp sugar
1 tbsp Chinese rice wine or dry sherry
2 spring onions, finely shredded
a few drops sesame oil
chilli sauce, to serve (optional)

**1** Cook the noodles in boiling water according to the instructions on the packet, then drain and rinse under cold water. Drain again then toss with 1 tablespoon of the oil.

**2** Slice the pork into thin shreds and trim the beans.

**3** Heat 3 tablespoons of the oil in a preheated wok until hot. Add the noodles and stir-fry for 2–3 minutes with 1 tablespoon of the soy sauce, then remove to a serving dish. Keep warm.

**4** Heat the remaining oil and stir-fry the beans and meat for 2 minutes. Add the salt, sugar, rice wine, the remaining soy sauce and about half of the spring onions to the wok.

**5** Stir the mixture in the wok, adding a little stock if necessary, then pour on top of the noodles, and sprinkle with sesame oil and the remaining spring onions.

**6** Serve the chow mein hot or cold with chilli sauce, if using.

# SPICED PUMPKIN SOUP

**SERVES 4**

2 tbsp olive oil
I onion, chopped
I garlic clove, chopped
I tbsp chopped fresh root ginger
I small red chilli, deseeded and finely chopped

2 tbsp chopped fresh coriander
I bay leaf
I kg/2 lb 4 oz pumpkin, peeled, deseeded and diced
600 ml/I pint vegetable stock
salt and pepper
single cream, to garnish

**GRANDMA'S TIPS**

*Pumpkins are often tough-skinned and difficult to handle. The easiest way to prepare a pumpkin or squash is to cut it into quarters using a sharp knife, then remove the seeds and cut into smaller pieces. These pieces will then be easier to peel, either using a sharp knife or a potato peeler. Occasionally you might find some prepared pumpkin in the supermarket, which makes things easier still.*

**1** Heat the oil in a saucepan over a medium heat. Add the onion and garlic and cook, stirring, for about 4 minutes, until slightly softened. Add the ginger, chilli, coriander, bay leaf and pumpkin and cook for another 3 minutes.

**2** Pour in the stock and bring to the boil. Using a slotted spoon, skim any scum from the surface. Reduce the heat and simmer gently, stirring occasionally, for about 25 minutes, or until the pumpkin is tender. Remove from the heat, take out the bay leaf and leave to cool a little.

**3** Transfer the soup into a food processor and blend until smooth (you may have to do this in batches). Return the mixture to the pan and season with salt and pepper. Reheat gently, stirring. Remove from the heat, pour into 4 warmed soup bowls, garnish each one with a swirl of cream and serve.

# FESTIVE BEEF
# WELLINGTON

**SERVES 4**

750 g/1 lb 10 oz thick beef fillet
2 tbsp butter
salt and pepper
2 tbsp vegetable oil
1 garlic clove, chopped

1 onion, chopped
175 g/6 oz chestnut mushrooms
1 tbsp chopped fresh sage
350 g/12 oz frozen puff pastry, defrosted
1 egg, beaten

**1** Preheat the oven to 220°C/425°F/Gas Mark 7. Put the beef in a roasting tin, spread with butter and season with salt and pepper. Roast for 30 minutes, then remove from the oven. Meanwhile, heat the oil in a pan over a medium heat. Add the garlic and onion and cook, stirring, for 3 minutes. Stir in the mushrooms, sage and salt and pepper to taste and cook for 5 minutes. Remove from the heat.

**2** Roll out the pastry into a rectangle large enough to enclose the beef, then place the beef in the middle and spread the mushroom mixture over it. Bring the long sides of the pastry together over the beef and seal with beaten egg. Tuck the short ends over (trim away excess pastry) and seal. Place on a baking sheet, seam-side down. Make 2 slits in the top. Decorate with dough shapes and brush with beaten egg. Bake for 40 minutes. If the pastry browns too quickly, cover with foil. Remove from the oven, cut into thick slices and serve hot.

# RACK OF LAMB

**SERVES 2**
1 trimmed rack of lamb, weighing
   250–300 g/9–10½ oz
1 garlic clove, crushed
150 ml/5 fl oz red wine
1 fresh rosemary sprig, crushed to
   release the flavour
salt and pepper
1 tbsp olive oil
150 ml/5 fl oz lamb stock
2 tbsp redcurrant jelly

**for the mint sauce**
bunch fresh mint leaves
2 tsp caster sugar
2 tbsp boiling water
2 tbsp white wine vinegar

**GRANDMA'S TIPS**

*This is an ideal roast to make for just two people. For more, double or treble the quantity. It makes a very good dinner party dish and is easy to carve. Serve with a mixture of spring vegetables and garnish with rosemary.*

**1** Place the rack of lamb in a non-metallic bowl and rub all over with the garlic. Pour over the wine and place the rosemary sprig on top. Cover and leave to marinate in the refrigerator for 3 hours or overnight if possible.

**2** Preheat the oven to 220°C/425°F/Gas Mark 7. Remove the lamb from the marinade, reserving the marinade. Pat the meat dry with kitchen paper and season well with salt and pepper. Place it in a small roasting tin, drizzle with the oil and roast for 15–20 minutes, depending on whether you like your meat pink or medium. Remove the lamb from the oven and leave to rest, covered with foil, in a warm place for 5 minutes.

**3** Meanwhile, pour the reserved marinade into a small saucepan, bring to the boil over a medium heat and boil rapidly for 5 minutes. Add the stock and redcurrant jelly and simmer, stirring, until the mixture is syrupy.

**4** To make the mint sauce, chop the fresh mint leaves and mix together with the sugar in a small bowl. Add the boiling water and stir to dissolve the sugar. Add the white wine vinegar and leave to stand for 30 minutes before serving with the lamb.

**5** Carve the lamb into cutlets and serve on warmed plates with the sauce spooned over the top. Serve the mint sauce separately.

# HERBED SALMON WITH HOLLANDAISE SAUCE

**SERVES 4**
4 salmon fillets, about 175 g/6 oz each,
  skin removed
salt and pepper
2 tbsp olive oil
1 tbsp chopped fresh dill
1 tbsp chopped fresh chives, plus extra
  for garnish

**for the hollandaise sauce**
3 egg yolks
1 tbsp water
salt and pepper
225 g/8 oz butter, cut into small cubes
juice of 1 lemon

**to serve**
freshly boiled new potatoes
freshly cooked broccoli
sesame seeds, for sprinkling (optional)

**GRANDMA'S TIPS**

*Hollandaise is a difficult sauce to make, as tends to separate. To simplify, boil the water with the lemon juice in a small pan. Place the egg yolks with the salt in a liquidiser and blend. With the motor running, pour the lemon juice mixture onto the egg yolks and blend. Melt the butter and add it to the blender in a steady stream until the mixture is thick. Hollandaise sauce should be served immediately after it has been made.*

1  Preheat the grill to medium. Rinse the fish fillets under cold running water and pat dry with kitchen paper. Season with salt and pepper. Combine the olive oil with the dill and chives, then brush the mixture over the fish. Transfer to the grill and cook for about 6–8 minutes, turning once and brushing with more oil and herb mixture, until cooked to your taste.

2  Meanwhile, to make the hollandaise sauce, put the egg yolks in a heatproof bowl over a pan of boiling water (or use a double boiler). Add the water and season with salt and pepper. Lower the heat and simmer, whisking constantly, until the mixture begins to thicken. Whisk in the butter, cube by cube, until the mixture is thick and shiny. Whisk in the lemon juice, then remove from the heat.

3  Remove the fish from the grill and transfer to individual serving plates. Pour over the sauce and garnish with chopped fresh chives. Serve with freshly boiled new potatoes and broccoli, and sprinkle with sesame seeds, if using.

# MIXED NUT ROAST
# WITH CRANBERRY &
# RED WINE SAUCE

**SERVES 4**

2 tbsp butter, plus extra for greasing
2 garlic cloves, chopped
1 large onion, chopped
50 g/1¾ oz pine kernels, toasted
75 g/2¾ oz hazelnuts, toasted
50 g/1¾ oz walnuts, ground
50 g/1¾ oz cashew nuts, ground
100 g/3½ oz wholemeal breadcrumbs
1 egg, lightly beaten

2 tbsp chopped fresh thyme
250 ml/9 fl oz vegetable stock
salt and pepper
sprigs of fresh thyme, to garnish

**for the cranberry & red wine sauce**
175 g/6 oz fresh cranberries
100 g/3½ oz caster sugar
300 ml/10 fl oz red wine
1 cinnamon stick

1  Preheat the oven to 180°C/350°F/Gas Mark 4. Grease a loaf tin and line it with greaseproof paper. Melt the butter in a saucepan over a medium heat. Add the garlic and onion and cook, stirring, for about 3 minutes. Remove the pan from the heat. Grind the pine kernels and hazelnuts. Stir all the nuts into the pan and add the breadcrumbs, egg, thyme, stock and seasoning.

2  Spoon the mixture into the loaf tin and level the surface. Cook in the centre of the preheated oven for 30 minutes or until cooked through and golden. The loaf is cooked when a skewer inserted into the centre comes out clean. Halfway through the cooking time, make the cranberry and red wine sauce. Put all the ingredients in a saucepan and bring to the boil. Reduce the heat and simmer, stirring occasionally, for 15 minutes.

3  Remove the nut roast from the oven and turn out. Garnish with sprigs of thyme and serve with the cranberry and red wine sauce.

# PERFECT ROAST
# POTATOES

**SERVES 6**
1.3 kg/3 lb large floury potatoes, such as
King Edwards, Maris Piper or Desirée,
peeled and cut into even-sized chunks

salt
3 tbsp goose fat, duck fat or olive oil

**GRANDMA'S TIPS**

*The potatoes can be seasoned
while they're roasting, which
allows the flavours to be
absorbed. Parsnips can also be
roasted in the same way but
they'll only need 2–3 minutes'
precooking and they don't need
to be shaken in the pan.*

**1** Preheat the oven to 220°C/425°F/Gas Mark 7.

**2** Cook the potatoes in a large saucepan of lightly salted boiling water over a medium heat, covered, for 5–7 minutes. They will still be firm. Remove from the heat. Meanwhile, add the fat to a roasting tin and place in the hot oven.

**3** Drain the potatoes well and return them to the saucepan. Cover with the lid and firmly shake the pan so that the surface of the potatoes is slightly roughened to help give a much crisper texture.

**4** Remove the roasting tin from the oven and carefully tip the potatoes into the hot fat. Baste them to ensure that they are all coated with it.

**5** Roast the potatoes at the top of the oven for 45–50 minutes until they are browned all over and thoroughly crisp. Turn the potatoes and baste again only once during the process or the crunchy edges will be destroyed.

**6** Using a slotted spoon, carefully transfer the potatoes from the roasting tin into a warmed serving dish. Sprinkle with a little salt and serve immediately. Any leftovers (although this is most unlikely) are delicious cold.

# GLAZED TURNIPS

**SERVES 4–6**
900 g/2 lb young turnips, peeled and
    quartered
salt and pepper
55 g/2 oz butter

1 tbsp brown sugar
150 ml/5 fl oz vegetable stock
1 sprig of fresh rosemary
chopped fresh parsley and grated orange
    rind, to garnish

**GRANDMA'S TIPS**

*As a variation, cook the turnips in a saucepan of boiling water for 20–25 minutes, or until tender. Drain well. Place the juice and grated rind of 1 orange and 1 tablespoon of honey in the rinsed-out saucepan and reduce until thick. Add the cooked turnips and toss to glaze. This dish is particularly delicious served with duck.*

1 Put the turnips into a saucepan of boiling salted water, bring back to the boil and simmer for 10 minutes. Drain well.

2 Melt the butter in the rinsed-out saucepan over a gentle heat, add the turnips and sugar and mix to coat well.

3 Add the stock with the rosemary and bring to the boil. Reduce the heat and simmer for 15–20 minutes with the lid off the pan so that the juices reduce and the turnips are tender and well glazed.

4 Remove the pan from the heat, discard the rosemary and season with salt and pepper to taste.

5 Serve immediately garnished with the chopped parsley and grated orange rind.

# ROASTED ROOT VEGETABLES

**SERVES 4–6**

3 parsnips, cut into 5-cm/2-inch chunks
4 baby turnips, quartered
3 carrots, cut into 5-cm/2-inch chunks
450 g/1 lb butternut squash, peeled and cut into 5-cm/2-inch chunks
450 g/1 lb sweet potatoes, peeled and cut into 5-cm/2-inch chunks

2 garlic cloves, finely chopped
2 tbsp chopped fresh rosemary
2 tbsp chopped fresh thyme
2 tsp chopped fresh sage
3 tbsp olive oil
salt and pepper
2 tbsp chopped fresh mixed herbs, such as parsley, thyme and mint, to garnish

**1** Preheat the oven to 220°C/425°F/Gas Mark 7.

**2** Arrange all the vegetables in a single layer in a large roasting tin. Scatter over the garlic and the herbs. Pour over the oil and season well with salt and pepper.

**3** Toss all the ingredients together until they are well mixed and coated with the oil (you can leave them to marinate at this stage to allow the flavours to be absorbed).

**4** Roast the vegetables at the top of the oven for 50–60 minutes until they are cooked and nicely browned. Turn the vegetables over halfway through the cooking time.

**5** Serve with a good handful of fresh herbs scattered on top and a final sprinkling of salt and pepper to taste.

# HONEYED PARSNIPS

**SERVES 4**
8 parsnips, peeled and quartered
4 tbsp vegetable oil
I tbsp honey

**GRANDMA'S TIPS**

*For a change try substituting maple syrup for the honey or use a mixture of root vegetables for a colourful dish.*

1 Preheat the oven to 180°C/350°F/Gas Mark 4.

2 Bring a large saucepan of water to the boil. Reduce the heat, add the parsnips and cook for 5 minutes. Drain thoroughly.

3 Pour 2 tablespoons of the oil into a shallow, ovenproof dish and add the parsnips. Mix the remaining oil with the honey and drizzle over the parsnips. Roast in the preheated oven for 45 minutes until golden brown and tender. Remove from the oven and serve.

# BRUSSELS SPROUTS WITH BUTTERED CHESTNUTS

**SERVES 4**
350 g/12 oz Brussels sprouts, trimmed
3 tbsp butter
100 g/3½ oz canned whole chestnuts

pinch of nutmeg
salt and pepper
50 g/1¾ oz flaked almonds, to garnish

**GRANDMA'S TIPS**

*Take care when buying canned chestnuts not to buy the sweetened ones. Instead of canned chestnuts, try vacuum packed ones, which are easy to find and use. Dried chestnuts are available from health food shops but they'll need a good soaking, preferably overnight, before use.*

**1** Bring a large saucepan of water to the boil. Add the Brussels sprouts and cook for 5 minutes. Drain thoroughly.

**2** Melt the butter in a large saucepan over a medium heat. Add the Brussels sprouts and cook, stirring, for 3 minutes, then add the chestnuts and nutmeg. Season with salt and pepper and stir well. Cook for another 2 minutes, stirring, then remove from the heat. Transfer to a serving dish, scatter over the almonds and serve.

# HONEY-GLAZED
# RED CABBAGE WITH
# SULTANAS

**SERVES 4**

2 tbsp butter
1 garlic clove, chopped
650 g/1 lb 7 oz red cabbage, shredded

150 g/5½ oz sultanas
1 tbsp honey
100 ml/3½ fl oz red wine
100 ml/3½ fl oz water

1  Melt the butter in a large saucepan over a medium heat. Add the garlic and cook, stirring, for 1 minute, until slightly softened.

2  Add the cabbage and sultanas, then stir in the honey. Cook for another minute. Pour in the wine and water and bring to the boil. Reduce the heat, cover and simmer, stirring occasionally, for about 45 minutes or until the cabbage is cooked. Serve hot.

# FESTIVE SHERRY TRIFLE

**SERVES 8**

**for the fruit layer**
100 g/3½ oz trifle sponges
150 ml/5 fl oz strawberry jam
250 ml/9 fl oz sherry
150 g/5½ oz fresh strawberries, hulled
   and sliced
400 g/14 oz canned mixed fruit, drained
1 large banana, sliced

**for the custard layer**
6 egg yolks
50 g/1¾ oz caster sugar
500 ml/18 fl oz milk
1 tsp vanilla essence

**for the topping**
300 ml/10 fl oz double cream
1–2 tbsp caster sugar
chocolate curls or flakes, to decorate

**GRANDMA'S TIPS**

*Instead of trifle sponges, you
could use macaroon biscuits,
sponge fingers or even sliced
Swiss roll. For an even more
exotic flavour, try substituting
Cassis or Framboise liqueur for
the sherry.*

1 Spread the trifle sponges with jam, cut them into bite-sized cubes and arrange in the bottom of a large glass serving bowl. Pour over the sherry and leave for 30 minutes.

2 Combine the strawberries, canned fruit and banana and arrange over the sponges. Cover with clingfilm and chill for 30 minutes.

3 To make the custard, put the egg yolks and sugar into a bowl and whisk together. Pour the milk into a pan and warm gently over a low heat. Remove from the heat and gradually stir into the egg mixture, then return the mixture to the pan and stir constantly over a low heat until thickened. Do not boil. Remove from the heat, pour into a bowl and stir in the vanilla. Cool for 1 hour. Spread the custard over the trifle sponge and fruit mixture, cover with clingfilm and chill for 2 hours.

4 To make the topping, whip the cream in a bowl and stir in sugar to taste. Spread over the trifle, then scatter over the chocolate. Cover with clingfilm and refrigerate for at least 2 hours before serving.

# FESTIVE MINCE PIES

**MAKES 12**

200 g/7 oz plain flour, plus extra for
  dusting
100 g/3½ oz butter
25 g/1 oz icing sugar

1 egg yolk
2–3 tbsp milk
300 g/10½ oz mincemeat
1 egg, beaten, for sealing and glazing
icing sugar, for dusting

**1** Preheat the oven to 180°C/350°F/Gas Mark 4. Sift the flour into a mixing bowl. Using your fingertips, rub in the butter until the mixture resembles breadcrumbs. Mix in the sugar and egg yolk.

**2** Stir in enough milk to make a soft dough, turn out onto a lightly floured work surface and knead lightly until smooth.

**3** Shape the dough into a ball and roll out to a thickness of 1 cm/½ inch. Use pastry cutters to cut out 12 rounds of 7 cm/2¾ inches diameter for the bases and 12 smaller star shapes for the tops. Dust 12 tartlet tins with flour and line with the dough rounds. Prick the bases with a fork, then half-fill each pie with mincemeat. Place the star shapes on top then brush all over with beaten egg. Bake in the preheated oven for 15 minutes. Remove from the oven and cool on a wire rack. Dust with icing sugar and serve.

# SPICED CHRISTMAS
# PUNCH

**SERVES 10**
1 litre/1¾ pints of red wine
4 tbsp sugar
1 cinnamon stick
400 ml/14 fl oz boiling water
100 ml/3½ fl oz brandy
100 ml/3½ fl oz sherry

100 ml/3½ fl oz orange liqueur, such as
  Cointreau
2 seedless oranges, cut into wedges
2 dessert apples, cored and cut into
  wedges

**GRANDMA'S TIPS**
*You should use heatproof glasses
to serve this hot punch. If you
are concerned that your glasses
may be too fragile, place a metal
teaspoon in each glass as you
pour so that some of the heat is
absorbed by the metal.*

1 Put the wine, sugar and cinnamon into a large saucepan and stir together well. Warm over a low heat, stirring, until just starting to simmer, but do not let it boil. Remove from the heat and strain through a sieve. Discard the cinnamon stick.

2 Return the wine to the pan and stir in the water, brandy, sherry and orange liqueur. Add the orange and apple wedges and warm gently over a very low heat, but do not let it boil. Remove from the heat and pour into a large, heatproof punch bowl. Ladle into heatproof glasses and serve hot.

*Those with a sweet tooth will fondly remember the delicious aromas of puddings and desserts that would emanate from Grandma's kitchen. Some are really quick and easy to assemble, whilst others take more time, making them best reserved for special occasions and family get-togethers. Chocolate mousse is always popular and, together with profiteroles, banana splits and Black Forest gateau, will give even the most chocoholic cook enough recipes to indulge in. Pies, strudels and crumbles are included to add fruit to the menu – the*

# GRANDMA'S JUST DESSERTS

*fruit can be changed according to taste and season, providing even more diversity. Along with the traditional favourites, such as baked apples, bread and butter pudding and good old rice pudding, you will find recipes for more exotic – but equally well-loved – desserts like Italian tiramisu, Mississippi mud pie and an American-style baked cheesecake. These are dishes that we've grown up with and adopted as our own, despite their far-flung origins. With such a wide selection you are certainly going to be spoilt for choice when it comes to choosing your Grandma's just dessert.*

# APPLE PIE

**SERVES 6**
**for the pastry**
350 g/12 oz plain flour
pinch of salt
85 g/3 oz butter or margarine, cut into
  small pieces
85 g/3 oz lard or white vegetable fat,
  cut into small pieces
about 6 tbsp cold water
beaten egg or milk, for glazing

**for the filling**
750 g–1 kg/1 lb 10 oz–2 lb 4 oz cooking
  apples, peeled, cored and sliced
125 g/4½ oz caster sugar, plus extra for
  sprinkling
½–1 tsp ground cinnamon, mixed spice
  or ground ginger
1–2 tbsp water (optional)

**GRANDMA'S TIPS**

*When preparing your apples make sure you prepare them one at a time, rather than peeling them all and then slicing them. Place the apple slices in a bowl of water to which has been added the juice of 1 lemon as you go along – this will stop them from discolouring.*

**1** To make the pastry, sift the flour and salt into a mixing bowl. Add the butter and lard and rub in with your fingertips until the mixture resembles fine breadcrumbs. Add the water and gather the mixture together into a dough. Wrap the dough and chill in the refrigerator for 30 minutes.

**2** Preheat the oven to 220°C/425°F/Gas Mark 7. Roll out almost two-thirds of the pastry thinly and use to line a deep 23-cm/9-inch pie plate or pie tin.

**3** Mix the apples with the sugar and spice and pack into the pastry case; the filling can come up above the rim. Add the water if needed, particularly if the apples are not very juicy.

**4** Roll out the remaining pastry to form a lid. Dampen the edges of the pie rim with water and position the lid, pressing the edges firmly together. Trim and crimp the edges.

**5** Use the trimmings to cut out leaves or other shapes to decorate the top of the pie, dampen and attach. Glaze the top of the pie with beaten egg or milk, make 1–2 slits in the top and place the pie on a baking sheet.

**6** Bake in the preheated oven for 20 minutes, then reduce the temperature to 180°C/350°F/Gas Mark 4 and bake for a further 30 minutes, or until the pastry is a light golden brown. Serve hot or cold, sprinkled with sugar.

# LATTICED CHERRY PIE

**SERVES 8**
**for the pastry**
140 g/5 oz plain flour, plus extra for
   dusting
¼ tsp baking powder
½ tsp mixed spice
½ tsp salt
50 g/1¾ oz caster sugar
55 g/2 oz cold unsalted butter, diced,
   plus extra for greasing
1 beaten egg, plus extra for glazing
water, for sealing

**for the filling**
900 g/2 lb stoned fresh cherries, or
   canned cherries, drained
150 g/5½ oz caster sugar
½ tsp almond essence
2 tsp cherry brandy
¼ tsp mixed spice
2 tbsp cornflour
2 tbsp water
25 g/1 oz unsalted butter

freshly whipped cream or ice cream,
   to serve

**GRANDMA'S TIPS**

*This pie can be made using other
fruits, such as blackberries. To
complement the blackberries,
substitute 2 teaspoons of cassis
liqueur for the cherry brandy.*

**1**  To make the pastry, sift the flour with the baking powder into a large bowl. Stir in the mixed spice, salt and sugar. Using your fingertips, rub in the butter until the mixture resembles fine breadcrumbs, then make a well in the centre. Pour the beaten egg into the well. Mix with a wooden spoon, then shape the mixture into a dough. Cut the dough in half, and use your hands to roll each half into a ball. Wrap the dough and chill in the refrigerator for 30 minutes.

**2**  Preheat the oven to 220°C/425°F/Gas Mark 7. Grease a 23-cm/9-inch round pie dish with butter. Roll out the pastry into 2 rounds, each 30 cm/12 inches in diameter. Use one to line the pie dish. Trim the edges, leaving an overhang of 1 cm/½ inch.

**3**  To make the filling, put half of the cherries and the sugar in a large saucepan. Bring to a simmer over a low heat, stirring, for 5 minutes, or until the sugar has melted. Stir in the almond essence, brandy and mixed spice. In a separate bowl, mix the cornflour and water to form a paste. Remove the saucepan from the heat, stir in the cornflour paste, then return to the heat and stir constantly until the mixture boils and thickens. Leave to cool a little. Stir in the remaining cherries, pour into the pastry case, then dot with butter.

**4**  Cut the remaining pastry round into long strips 1 cm/½ inch wide. Lay the strips evenly on the top of the filling, crisscrossing to form a lattice. Trim off the ends and seal the edges with water. Use your fingers to crimp around the rim, then brush the top with beaten egg to glaze. Cover with kitchen foil, then bake for 30 minutes. Remove from the oven, discard the foil, then return the pie to the oven for a further 15 minutes, or until cooked and golden. Serve warm with freshly whipped cream or ice cream.

# RHUBARB CRUMBLE

**SERVES 6**
900 g/2 lb rhubarb
115 g/4 oz caster sugar
grated rind and juice of 1 orange
cream, yogurt or custard, to serve

**for the crumble**
225 g/8 oz plain or wholemeal flour
115 g/4 oz butter
115 g/4 oz soft brown sugar
1 tsp ground ginger

1  Preheat the oven to 190°C/375°F/Gas Mark 5.

2  Cut the rhubarb into 2.5-cm/1-inch lengths and place in a 1.7-litre/3-pint ovenproof dish with the sugar and the orange rind and juice.

3  Make the crumble by placing the flour in a mixing bowl and rubbing in the butter until the mixture resembles breadcrumbs. Stir in the sugar and the ginger.

4  Spread the crumble evenly over the fruit and press down lightly using a fork.

5  Bake in the centre of the oven on a baking tray for 25–30 minutes until the crumble is golden brown.

6  Serve warm with cream, yogurt or custard.

# LEMON MERINGUE PIE

**SERVES 4**
**for the pastry**
150 g/5½ oz plain flour, plus extra for
   dusting
85 g/3 oz butter, cut into small pieces,
   plus extra for greasing
35 g/1¼ oz icing sugar, sifted
finely grated rind of ½ lemon
½ egg yolk, beaten
1½ tbsp milk

**for the filling**
3 tbsp cornflour
300 ml/10 fl oz water
juice and grated rind of 2 lemons
175 g/6 oz caster sugar
2 eggs, separated

## GRANDMA'S TIPS

*This dessert is usually served cold, but why not try it hot? It may sound rather decadent but hot lemon meringue pie with cold ice cream is to die for. Lime or orange juice and rind may be substituted for the lemon juice and rind for a change.*

**1** To make the pastry, sift the flour into a bowl. Rub in the butter with your fingertips until the mixture resembles fine breadcrumbs. Mix in the remaining ingredients. Knead briefly on a lightly floured work surface. Rest for 30 minutes.

**2** Preheat the oven to 180°C/350°F/Gas Mark 4. Grease a 20-cm/8-inch pie dish with butter. Roll out the pastry to a thickness of 5 mm/¼ inch; use it to line the base and sides of the dish. Prick all over with a fork, line with baking paper and fill with baking beans. Bake for 15 minutes. Remove the pastry case from the oven and take out the paper and beans. Reduce the temperature to 150°C/300°F/Gas Mark 2.

**3** To make the filling, mix the cornflour with a little of the water. Put the remaining water in a saucepan. Stir in the lemon juice and rind and cornflour paste. Bring to the boil, stirring.

**4** Cook for 2 minutes. Cool a little. Stir in 5 tablespoons of the sugar and the egg yolks and pour into the pastry case.

**5** Whisk the egg whites in a clean, grease-free bowl until stiff. Gradually whisk in the remaining sugar and spread over the pie. Bake for a further 40 minutes. Remove from oven, cool and serve.

# MISSISSIPPI MUD PIE

**SERVES 8**

**for the pastry**
225 g/8 oz plain flour, plus extra for
  dusting
2 tbsp cocoa powder
140 g/5 oz butter
2 tbsp caster sugar
1–2 tbsp cold water

**for the filling**
175 g/6 oz butter
350 g/12 oz soft dark brown sugar

4 eggs, lightly beaten
4 tbsp cocoa powder, sifted
150 g/5½ oz plain chocolate
300 ml/10 fl oz single cream
1 tsp chocolate essence

**to decorate**
425 ml/15 fl oz double cream, whipped
chocolate flakes and curls

**1** To make the pastry, sift the flour and cocoa powder into a mixing bowl. Rub in the butter with your fingertips until the mixture resembles fine breadcrumbs. Stir in the sugar and enough cold water to mix to a soft dough. Wrap the dough and chill in the refrigerator for 15 minutes.

**2** Preheat the oven to 190°C/375°F/Gas Mark 5. Roll out the pastry on a lightly floured work surface and use to line a 23-cm/9-inch loose-based flan tin or ceramic flan dish. Line with baking paper and fill with baking beans. Bake in the preheated oven for 15 minutes. Remove the paper and beans from the pastry case and cook for a further 10 minutes until crisp.

**3** To make the filling, beat the butter and sugar together in a bowl and gradually beat in the eggs with the cocoa powder. Melt the chocolate and beat it into the mixture with the single cream and the chocolate essence.

**4** Reduce the oven temperature to 160°C/325°F/Gas Mark 3. Pour the mixture into the pastry case and bake for 45 minutes, or until the filling has set gently.

**5** Let the mud pie cool completely, then transfer the pie to a serving plate, if you like. Cover with the whipped cream.

**6** Decorate the pie with chocolate flakes and curls and then chill until ready to serve.

# BREAD & BUTTER PUDDING

**SERVES 4–6**

85 g/3 oz butter, softened
6 slices of thick white bread
55 g/2 oz mixed fruit (sultanas, currants and raisins)
25 g/1 oz candied peel
3 large eggs

300 ml/10 fl oz milk
150 ml/5 fl oz double cream
55 g/2 oz caster sugar
whole nutmeg, for grating
1 tbsp demerara sugar
cream, to serve

**1** Preheat the oven to 180°C/350°F/Gas Mark 4.

**2** Use a little of the butter to grease a 20 x 25-cm/8 x 10-inch baking dish and butter the slices of bread. Cut the bread into quarters and arrange half overlapping in the dish.

**3** Scatter half the fruit and peel over the bread, cover with the remaining bread slices and add the remaining fruit and peel.

**4** In a mixing jug, whisk the eggs well and mix in the milk, cream and sugar. Pour this over the pudding and leave to stand for 15 minutes to allow the bread to soak up some of the egg mixture. Tuck in most of the fruit as you don't want it to burn in the oven. Grate the nutmeg over the top of the pudding, according to taste, and sprinkle over the demerara sugar.

**5** Place the pudding on a baking tray and bake at the top of the oven for 30–40 minutes until just set and golden brown.

**6** Remove from the oven and serve warm with a little pouring cream.

# BLACK FOREST
## GATEAU

**SERVES 8**

3 tbsp unsalted butter, melted, plus extra
   for greasing
900 g/2 lb fresh cherries, stoned and
   halved
250 g/9 oz caster sugar
100 ml/3½ fl oz cherry brandy
100 g/3½ oz plain flour

50 g/1¾ oz cocoa powder
½ tsp baking powder
4 eggs
1 litre/1¾ pints double cream

**to decorate**
grated dark chocolate
whole fresh cherries

**GRANDMA'S TIPS**

*It is possible to make this
extravagant gateau using canned
cherries – drain the fruit from
the juice and use the liquid to
soak the cake before assembling.
Kirsch or brandy can be used
instead of the cherry brandy.*

**1** Preheat the oven to 180°C/350°F/Gas Mark 4. Grease and line a 23-cm/9-inch
springform cake pan. Place the cherries in a saucepan, add 3 tablespoons of the sugar
and the cherry brandy and bring to a simmer over medium heat. Simmer for 5 minutes.
Drain, reserving the syrup. In a large bowl, sift together the flour, cocoa, and baking
powder.

**2** Place the eggs in a heatproof bowl and beat in 160 g/5¾ oz of the sugar. Place the
bowl over a saucepan of simmering water and beat for 6 minutes, or until thickened.
Remove from the heat, then gradually fold in the flour mixture and melted butter. Spoon
into the cake pan and bake for 40 minutes. Remove from the oven and leave to cool in
the pan.

**3** Turn out the cake and cut in half horizontally. Mix the double cream and the
remaining sugar together and whip lightly until soft peaks form. Spread the reserved
syrup over the cut sides of the cake, then spread a layer of whipped cream on the
bottom half of the cake, followed by the cherries, and then place the other half on top.
Cover the top of the cake with whipped cream, sprinkle over the grated chocolate and
decorate with whole fresh cherries.

# PROFITEROLES

**SERVES 4**
**for the choux pastry**
5 tbsp butter, plus extra for greasing
200 ml/7 fl oz cold water
100 g/3½ oz plain flour
3 eggs, beaten

**for the cream filling**
300 ml/10 fl oz double cream
3 tbsp caster sugar
1 tsp vanilla essence

**for the chocolate & brandy sauce**
125 g/4½ oz plain dark chocolate,
    broken into pieces
2½ tbsp butter
6 tbsp water
2 tbsp brandy

1  Preheat the oven to 200°C/400°F/Gas Mark 6.

2  Grease a large baking sheet with butter. To make the pastry, place the water and butter in a saucepan and bring to the boil. Meanwhile, sift the flour into a bowl. Remove the saucepan from the heat and beat in the flour until smooth. Cool for 5 minutes. Beat in enough of the eggs to give the mixture a soft, dropping consistency. Transfer to a piping bag fitted with a 1-cm/½-inch plain nozzle. Pipe small balls onto the baking sheet. Bake for 25 minutes. Remove from the oven. Pierce each ball with a skewer to let steam escape.

3  To make the filling, whip together the cream, sugar and vanilla essence. Cut the pastry balls almost in half, then fill with the cream filling.

4  To make the sauce, gently melt the chocolate and butter with the water in a small saucepan, stirring, until smooth. Stir in the brandy. Pile the profiteroles into individual serving dishes or into a pyramid on a raised cake stand. Pour over the sauce and serve.

# CHOCOLATE MOUSSE

**SERVES 4**
300 g/10½ oz plain dark chocolate
1 ½ tbsp unsalted butter
1 tbsp brandy
4 eggs, separated
cocoa powder, for dusting

**1** Break the chocolate into small pieces and place in a heatproof bowl set over a pan of simmering water. Add the butter and melt with the chocolate, stirring, until smooth. Remove from the heat, stir in the brandy and leave to cool slightly. Add the egg yolks and beat until smooth.

**2** In a separate bowl, whisk the egg whites until stiff peaks have formed, then fold them into the chocolate mixture. Spoon the mixture into 4 small serving bowls and level the surfaces. Transfer to the refrigerator and chill for at least 4 hours until set.

**3** Take the mousse out of the refrigerator, dust with cocoa powder and serve.

# TRADITIONAL
## TIRAMISU

**SERVES 6**

20–24 sponge fingers, about 150 g/5½ oz
2 tbsp cold black coffee
2 tbsp coffee essence
2 tbsp almond liqueur
4 egg yolks
85 g/3 oz caster sugar
a few drops of vanilla essence

grated rind of ½ lemon
350 g/12 oz mascarpone cheese
2 tsp lemon juice
250 ml/9 fl oz double cream
1 tbsp milk
25 g/1 oz lightly toasted flaked almonds
2 tbsp cocoa powder
1 tbsp icing sugar

**GRANDMA'S TIPS**

*This wonderful Italian dessert – a literal translation is 'pick me up' – is very rich and should be served in small portions. A glass of Amaretto is the perfect accompaniment. This dessert looks equally as divine when served in individual ramekins – divide the ingredients accordingly for mouth-watering results.*

1  Arrange almost half of the sponge fingers in the base of a serving dish. Place the black coffee, coffee essence and almond liqueur in a bowl and mix. Sprinkle just over half of the mixture over the sponge fingers.

2  Place the egg yolks in a heatproof bowl with the sugar, vanilla essence and lemon rind. Stand the bowl over a saucepan of gently simmering water and whisk until very thick and creamy and the whisk leaves a heavy trail when lifted from the bowl.

3  Place the mascarpone cheese in a separate bowl with the lemon juice and beat until smooth. Stir into the egg mixture and, when evenly blended, pour half of the mixture over the sponge fingers and spread out evenly.

4  Add another layer of sponge fingers, sprinkle with the remaining coffee mixture, then cover with the rest of the cheese and egg mixture. Leave to chill in the refrigerator for at least 2 hours, preferably overnight.

5  Whip the cream and milk together until fairly stiff and spread or pipe over the dessert. Sprinkle with the flaked almonds, then sift an even layer of cocoa powder over the top to cover completely. Finally, sift a layer of icing sugar over the cocoa powder and serve.

# BAKED RICE PUDDING

**SERVES 4–6**

1 tbsp melted unsalted butter
115 g/4 oz pudding rice
55 g/2 oz caster sugar
850 ml/1 ½ pints full-cream milk
½ tsp vanilla essence

40 g/1 ½ oz unsalted butter, chilled and
    cut into pieces
whole nutmeg, for grating
cream, jam, fresh fruit purée, stewed
    fruit, honey or ice cream, to serve

## GRANDMA'S TIPS

*In place of nutmeg, you can try grated lemon rind or another spice such as cinnamon to flavour the rice pudding. A handful of raisins or other dried fruit can be added before cooking. If you wish, the rice pudding may be cooked in individual ramekins – just reduce the cooking time to 1–1½ hours.*

1  Preheat the oven to 150°C/300°F/Gas Mark 2. Grease a 1.2-litre/2-pint baking dish (a gratin dish is good) with the melted butter, place the rice in the dish and sprinkle with the sugar.

2  Heat the milk in a saucepan until almost boiling, then pour over the rice. Add the vanilla essence and stir well to dissolve the sugar.

3  Cut the butter into small pieces and scatter over the surface of the pudding.

4  Grate the whole nutmeg over the top, using as much as you like to give a good covering.

5  Place the dish on a baking tray and bake in the centre of the oven for 1½–2 hours until the pudding is well browned on the top. You can stir it after the first half hour to disperse the rice.

6  Serve hot topped with cream, jam, fresh fruit purée, stewed fruit, honey or ice cream.

# BAKED APPLES

**SERVES 4**

25 g/1 oz blanched almonds
55 g/2 oz dried apricots
1 piece stem ginger, drained
1 tbsp clear honey

1 tbsp syrup from the stem ginger jar
4 tbsp rolled oats
4 large cooking apples

**1** Preheat the oven to 180°C/350°F/Gas Mark 4. Using a sharp knife, chop the almonds very finely. Chop the apricots and stem ginger very finely. Reserve.

**2** Place the honey and syrup in a saucepan and heat until the honey has melted. Stir in the oats and cook gently over a low heat for 2 minutes. Remove the saucepan from the heat and stir in the almonds, apricots and stem ginger.

**3** Core the apples, widen the tops slightly and score around the circumference of each to prevent the skins bursting during cooking. Place them in an ovenproof dish and fill the cavities with the stuffing. Pour just enough water into the dish to come about one-third of the way up the apples. Bake in the preheated oven for 40 minutes, or until tender. Serve immediately.

# BLUEBERRY PANCAKES

**MAKES 10–12**
140 g/5 oz plain flour
2 tbsp caster sugar
2 tbsp baking powder
½ tsp salt
225 ml/8 fl oz buttermilk
3 tbsp butter, melted

1 large egg
140 g/5 oz fresh blueberries, plus
   extra to serve
sunflower oil, for oiling
butter and warmed maple syrup,
   to serve

**GRANDMA'S TIPS**

*These small pancakes are ideal to serve for breakfast with crispy bacon or scrambled eggs and any other accompaniment of your choice.*

1 Preheat the oven to 140°C/275°F/Gas Mark 1. Sieve the flour, sugar, baking powder and salt together into a large bowl and make a well in the centre.

2 Beat the buttermilk, butter and egg together in a separate small bowl, then pour the mixture into the well in the dry ingredients. Beat the dry ingredients into the liquid, gradually drawing them in from the side, until a smooth batter is formed. Gently stir in the blueberries.

3 Heat a large frying pan over a medium-high heat until a splash of water dances on the surface. Using a pastry brush or crumpled piece of kitchen paper, oil the base of the frying pan.

4 Drop about 4 tablespoons of batter separately into the frying pan and spread each out into a 10-cm/4-inch round. Continue adding as many pancakes as will fit in your frying pan. Cook until small bubbles appear on the surface, then flip over with a spatula or palette knife and cook the pancakes on the other side for a further 1–2 minutes until golden brown.

5 Transfer the pancakes to a warmed plate and keep warm in the preheated oven while you cook the remaining batter, lightly oiling the frying pan as before. Make a stack of the pancakes with baking paper in between each pancake.

6 Serve with a knob of butter on top of each pancake and warm maple syrup for pouring over.

# BANANA SPLITS

**SERVES 4**
4 bananas
6 tbsp chopped mixed nuts, to serve

**for the vanilla ice cream**
300 ml/10 fl oz milk
1 tsp vanilla essence
3 egg yolks
100 g/3½ oz caster sugar
300 ml/10 fl oz double cream, whipped

**for the chocolate rum sauce**
125 g/4½ oz plain chocolate, broken into
   small pieces
2½ tbsp butter
6 tbsp water
1 tbsp rum

**GRANDMA'S TIPS**
*For a quick and easy pudding,
use shop-bought ice cream. If
you're serving the banana splits
to children, omit the rum from
the chocolate sauce.*

1  To make the ice cream, heat the milk and vanilla essence in a saucepan until almost boiling. In a bowl, beat together the egg yolks and sugar. Remove the milk from the heat and stir a little into the egg mixture. Transfer the mixture to the pan. Stir over a low heat until thick. Do not boil. Remove from the heat. Cool for 30 minutes, fold in the cream, cover with clingfilm and chill for 1 hour. Transfer into an ice-cream maker and process for 15 minutes. Alternatively, transfer into a freezerproof container and freeze for 1 hour, then place in a bowl and beat to break up the ice crystals. Put back in the container and freeze for 30 minutes. Repeat twice more, freezing for 30 minutes and whisking each time.

2  To make the sauce, melt the chocolate and butter with the water in a saucepan, stirring. Remove from the heat and stir in the rum. Peel the bananas, slice lengthways and arrange on 4 serving dishes. Top with ice cream and nuts and serve with the sauce.

Remember the smells of home-baked cakes, biscuits and scones when you were young? It was on those days that you learned to rub fat into flour with your fingertips to make pastry and to beat sugar and butter together to make cakes. It was fun to sprinkle flour over the kitchen table, roll out biscuit dough and cut it into different shapes – Grandma didn't seem to mind the mess. The best bit was eating the misshapen bits when they were still hot from the oven. This chapter provides recipes for all kinds of delicious goodies – from

# GRANDMA'S BAKING DAY

a classic Victoria sponge cake to indulgent chocolate brownies. Perhaps it will even encourage you to bake with your own children or grandchildren – they will particularly enjoy helping to make the easy nutty flapjacks or assembling the lemon butterfly cakes. All of the recipes in this section are perfect for filling those little gaps in the day, be it mid-morning or tea-time – but make sure you put the rest away in an airtight tin so that there is always something delicious to hand when friends or family come by.

# SANDWICH CAKE WITH CHOCOLATE TOPPING

**SERVES 8–10**
**for the cakes**
125 g/4½ oz soft margarine, plus extra
  for greasing
125 g/4½ oz caster sugar
2 eggs
1 tbsp golden syrup
125 g/4½ oz self-raising flour, sifted
2 tbsp cocoa powder, sifted

**for the filling and topping**
50 g/1¾ oz icing sugar, sifted
25 g/1 oz butter
100 g/3½ oz milk chocolate
a little white chocolate, melted
  (optional)

**GRANDMA'S TIPS**

*This simple chocolate-flavoured Victoria sandwich cake is a good base for all sorts of desserts. It is ideal as a birthday cake to decorate as you wish, or to serve with raspberries and cream for a summer dessert.*

1  Preheat the oven to 160°C/325°F/Gas Mark 3. Lightly grease two 18-cm/7-inch shallow cake tins.

2  Place all of the ingredients for the cake in a large mixing bowl and beat with a wooden spoon or electric hand whisk to form a smooth mixture.

3  Divide the mixture between the prepared tins and level the tops. Bake in the preheated oven for 20 minutes, or until springy to the touch. Cool for a few minutes in the tins before transferring to a wire rack to cool completely.

4  To make the filling, beat the icing sugar and butter together in a bowl until light and fluffy. Melt the milk chocolate and beat half into the filling mixture. Use the filling to sandwich the 2 cakes together.

5  Spread the remaining melted milk chocolate over the top of the cake. Pipe circles of contrasting melted white chocolate and feather into the milk chocolate with a cocktail stick, if liked. Leave to set before serving.

# VICTORIA SPONGE CAKE

**SERVES 8–10**

175 g/6 oz butter, at room temperature, plus extra for greasing
175 g/6 oz caster sugar
3 eggs, beaten

175 g/6 oz self-raising flour
pinch of salt
3 tbsp raspberry jam
1 tbsp caster or icing sugar

**GRANDMA'S TIPS**

*These cakes can also be flavoured with grated lemon rind and sandwiched together with lemon curd for a summery feel. For a simple butter cream filling, beat together equal quantities of butter and icing sugar until light and fluffy.*

**1** Preheat the oven to 180°C/350°F/Gas Mark 4.

**2** Grease two 20-cm/8-inch sponge tins and line with greaseproof paper or baking paper.

**3** Cream the butter and sugar together in a mixing bowl using a wooden spoon or a hand-held mixer until the mixture is pale in colour and light and fluffy.

**4** Add the egg a little at a time, beating well after each addition.

**5** Sift the flour and salt and carefully add to the mixture, folding it in with a metal spoon or a spatula.

**6** Divide the mixture between the tins and smooth over with the spatula.

**7** Place them on the same shelf in the centre of the oven and bake for 25–30 minutes until well risen, golden brown and beginning to shrink from the sides of the tin.

**8** Remove from the oven and allow to stand for 1 minute.

**9** Loosen the cakes from around the edge of the tins using a palette knife. Turn the cakes out onto a clean tea towel, remove the paper and invert them onto a wire rack (this prevents the wire rack from marking the top of the cakes).

**10** When completely cool, sandwich together with the jam and sprinkle with the sugar. The cake is delicious when freshly baked, but any remaining cake can be stored in an airtight tin for up to 1 week.

# LEMON DRIZZLE CAKE

**SERVES 8**
butter, for greasing
200 g/7 oz plain flour
2 tsp baking powder
200 g/7 oz caster sugar
4 eggs
150 ml/5 fl oz soured cream
grated rind of 1 large lemon
4 tbsp lemon juice
150 ml/5 fl oz sunflower oil

**for the syrup**
4 tbsp icing sugar
3 tbsp lemon juice

**1** Preheat the oven to 180°C/350°F/Gas Mark 4. Lightly grease a 20-cm/8-inch loose-bottom round cake tin and line the base with baking paper.

**2** Sieve the flour and baking powder into a mixing bowl and stir in the caster sugar.

**3** In a separate bowl, whisk the eggs, soured cream, lemon rind, lemon juice and oil together.

**4** Pour the egg mixture into the dry ingredients and mix well until evenly combined.

**5** Pour the mixture into the prepared tin and bake in the preheated oven for 45–60 minutes until risen and golden brown.

**6** Meanwhile, to make the syrup, mix together the icing sugar and lemon juice in a small saucepan. Stir over a low heat until just beginning to bubble and turn syrupy.

**7** As soon as the cake comes out of the oven, prick the surface with a fine skewer, then brush the syrup over the top. Leave the cake to cool completely in the tin before turning out and serving.

# RICH FRUIT CAKE

**SERVES 12**
butter, for greasing
175 g/6 oz stoned unsweetened dates
125 g/4½ oz ready-to-eat dried prunes
200 ml/7 fl oz unsweetened orange juice
2 tbsp black treacle
I tsp finely grated lemon rind
I tsp finely grated orange rind
225 g/8 oz wholemeal self-raising flour
I tsp mixed spice
125 g/4½ oz seedless raisins

125 g/4½ oz sultanas
125 g/4½ oz currants
125 g/4½ oz dried cranberries
3 large eggs, separated

**to decorate**
I tbsp apricot jam, warmed
icing sugar, for dusting
175 g/6 oz sugar paste
strips of orange rind
strips of lemon rind

1 Grease and line a deep 20-cm/8-inch round cake tin. Chop the dates and prunes and place in a large, heavy-based saucepan. Pour over the orange juice and simmer for 10 minutes. Remove the saucepan from the heat and beat the fruit mixture until puréed. Add the treacle and citrus rinds and leave to cool.

2 Preheat the oven to 160°C/325°F/Gas Mark 3. Sift the flour and mixed spice into a bowl, adding any bran that remains in the sieve. Add the raisins, sultanas, currants and dried cranberries. When the date and prune mixture is cool, whisk in the egg yolks. Whisk the egg whites in a clean bowl until stiff. Spoon the fruit mixture into the dry ingredients and mix together. Gently fold in the egg whites. Transfer to the prepared tin and bake in the preheated oven for 1½ hours. Leave to cool in the tin.

3 Remove the cake from the tin and brush the top with jam. Dust the work surface with icing sugar and roll out the sugar paste thinly. Lay the sugar paste over the top of the cake and trim the edges. Decorate with orange and lemon rind.

# CLASSIC CARROT CAKE

**SERVES 12**
butter, for greasing
125 g/4½ oz self-raising flour
pinch of salt
1 tsp ground cinnamon
125 g/4½ oz soft brown sugar
2 eggs
100 ml/3½ fl oz sunflower oil
125 g/4½ oz carrot, peeled and
   finely grated
25 g/1 oz desiccated coconut
25 g/1 oz walnuts, chopped
walnut pieces, to decorate

**for the icing**
50 g/1¾ oz butter, softened
50 g/1¾ oz soft cheese
225 g/8 oz icing sugar, sifted
1 tsp lemon juice

## GRANDMA'S TIPS

*This cake freezes well (without the icing) and can be kept for up to three months. It's perfect for a teatime treat as well as a quick dessert served with some ice cream.*

1 Preheat the oven to 180°C/350°F/Gas Mark 4. Lightly grease a 20-cm/8-inch square cake tin and line the base with baking paper.

2 Sift the flour, salt and ground cinnamon into a large bowl and stir in the brown sugar. Add the eggs and oil to the dry ingredients and mix well.

3 Stir in the grated carrot, desiccated coconut and chopped walnuts.

4 Pour the mixture into the prepared tin and bake in the preheated oven for 20–25 minutes, or until just firm to the touch. Leave to cool in the tin.

5 Meanwhile, make the icing. In a bowl, beat together the butter, soft cheese, icing sugar and lemon juice until the mixture is fluffy and creamy.

6 Turn the cake out of the tin and cut into 12 bars or slices. Spread with the icing and then decorate with walnut pieces.

# APPLE STREUSEL CAKE

**SERVES 8**
115 g/4 oz butter, plus extra for greasing
450 g/1 lb cooking apples
175 g/6 oz self-raising flour
1 tsp ground cinnamon
pinch of salt
115 g/4 oz caster sugar
2 eggs

1–2 tbsp milk
icing sugar, for dusting

**for the streusel topping**
115 g/4 oz self-raising flour
85 g/3 oz butter
85 g/3 oz caster sugar

**1**  Preheat the oven to 180°C/350°F/Gas Mark 4, then grease a 23-cm/9-inch springform cake tin. To make the streusel topping, sift the flour into a bowl and rub in the butter until the mixture resembles coarse crumbs. Stir in the sugar and reserve.

**2**  Peel, core and thinly slice the apples. To make the cake, sift the flour into a bowl with the cinnamon and salt. Place the butter and sugar in a separate bowl and beat together until light and fluffy. Gradually beat in the eggs, adding a little of the flour mixture with the last addition of egg. Gently fold in half the remaining flour mixture, then fold in the rest with the milk.

**3**  Spoon the mixture into the prepared tin and smooth the top. Cover with the sliced apples and sprinkle the streusel topping evenly over the top. Bake in the preheated oven for 1 hour, or until browned and firm to the touch. Leave to cool in the tin before opening the sides. Dust the cake with icing sugar before serving.

# COFFEE &
# WALNUT CAKE

**SERVES 8**
**for the icing**
6 tbsp cocoa powder
2 tbsp cornflour
6 tbsp caster sugar
125 ml/4 fl oz strong black coffee,
  cooled
250 ml/9 fl oz milk

walnut halves, to decorate

**for the sponge**
85 g/3 oz butter, softened, plus extra for
  greasing
275 g/9½ oz plain flour
1 tbsp baking powder
85 g/3 oz caster sugar
2 eggs
150 ml/5 fl oz milk
3 tbsp hot strong black coffee
60 g/2¼ oz shelled walnuts, chopped
50 g/1¾ oz sultanas

**GRANDMA'S TIPS**
*This soft-textured cake is always*
*very popular. The chocolate*
*topping can be replaced with*
*a simple sugar icing (made*
*with icing sugar and water) if*
*preferred.*

**1** To make the icing, put all the ingredients into a food processor and process until creamy. Transfer to a saucepan and heat, stirring, over a medium heat until bubbling. Cook for 1 minute, then pour into a heatproof bowl. Leave to cool, then cover with clingfilm and refrigerate for at least 2 hours.

**2** Preheat the oven to 190°C/375°F/Gas Mark 5. Grease a 23-cm/9-inch loose-bottomed cake tin with butter and line with baking paper. To make the sponge, sift the flour and baking powder into a bowl, then stir in the sugar. In a separate bowl, beat together the butter, eggs, milk and coffee, then mix into the flour mixture.

**3** Stir in the chopped walnuts and the sultanas. Spoon the mixture into the prepared cake tin and level the surface. Transfer to the preheated oven and bake for 1 hour. Remove from the oven and leave to cool. When cool enough to handle, turn out on to a wire rack and leave to cool completely. Spread the icing over the top of the cooled cake, decorate with the walnut halves and serve.

# GINGERBREAD

**MAKES 12–16**
450 g/1 lb plain flour
3 tsp baking powder
1 tsp bicarbonate of soda
3 tsp ground ginger
175 g/6 oz unsalted butter
175 g/6 oz soft brown sugar

175 g/6 oz black treacle
175 g/6 oz golden syrup
1 egg, beaten
300 ml/10 fl oz milk
cream or warmed golden syrup,
    to serve

**GRANDMA'S TIPS**

*A very moist gingerbread is a delight. It can be made even better by mixing in 55 g/2 oz chopped preserved stem ginger just before putting the mixture into the tin.*

1  Line a 23-cm/9-inch square cake tin, 5 cm/2 inches deep, with greaseproof or baking paper.

2  Preheat the oven to 160ºC/325ºF/Gas Mark 3.

3  Sift the flour, baking powder, bicarbonate of soda and ground ginger into a large mixing bowl.

4  Place the butter, sugar, treacle and syrup in a medium saucepan and heat over a low heat until the butter has melted and the sugar dissolved. Allow to cool a little.

5  Mix the beaten egg with the milk and add to the cooled syrup mixture.

6  Add all the liquid ingredients to the flour mixture and beat well using a wooden spoon until the mixture is smooth and glossy.

7  Pour the mixture into the prepared tin and bake in the centre of the oven for 1½ hours until well risen and just firm to the touch. This gives a lovely sticky gingerbread, but if you like a firmer cake cook for a further 15 minutes.

8  Remove from the oven and allow the cake to cool in the tin. When cool, remove the cake from the tin with the lining paper. Over wrap with foil and place in an airtight tin for up to 1 week to allow the flavours to mature.

9  Cut into wedges and serve cold with tea or coffee or warm with cream and golden syrup.

# BANANA LOAF

**SERVES 6**

unsalted butter, for greasing
125 g/4½ oz white self-raising flour
100 g/3½ oz light brown self-raising flour
150 g/5½ oz demerara sugar
pinch of salt
½ tsp ground cinnamon

½ tsp ground nutmeg
2 large ripe bananas, peeled
175 ml/6 fl oz orange juice
2 eggs, beaten
4 tbsp rapeseed oil
honey, to serve

**GRANDMA'S TIPS**

*This loaf is delicious simply buttered or served with chopped banana, walnuts and a drizzle of honey. Try toasting a slice or two the next day to bring out even more of the banana flavour.*

1 Preheat the oven to 180°C/350°F/Gas Mark 4. Lightly grease and line a 450-g/1-lb loaf tin.

2 Sift the flours, sugar, a pinch of salt, and the spices into a large bowl.

3 In a separate bowl, mash the bananas with the orange juice, then stir in the eggs and oil. Pour into the dry ingredients and mix well.

4 Spoon into the prepared loaf tin and bake in the preheated oven for 1 hour, then test to see if it is cooked by inserting a skewer into the centre. If it comes out clean, the loaf is done. If not, bake for a further 10 minutes and test again.

5 Remove from the oven and leave to cool in the tin. Turn the loaf out, slice and serve with honey.

# STRAWBERRY ROULADE

**SERVES 8**
3 large eggs
125 g/4½ oz caster sugar
125 g/4½ oz plain flour
1 tbsp hot water

**for the filling**
200 ml/7 fl oz low-fat fromage frais
1 tsp almond essence
225 g/8 oz small strawberries
15 g/½ oz flaked almonds, toasted
icing sugar, for dusting

**GRANDMA'S TIPS**

*Making a roulade looks quite difficult, but it really is quite simple when you use baking paper. Try varying the filling by using raspberries instead of the strawberries or whipped cream instead of the mascarpone. For a simple roulade, fill with jam – this makes a good base for a trifle.*

**1** Preheat the oven to 220°C/425°F/Gas Mark 7. Line a 35 x 25-cm/14 x 10-inch Swiss roll tin with baking paper. Place the eggs in a large, heatproof bowl with the caster sugar, place over a saucepan of hot water and, using an electric beater, beat until pale and thick.

**2** Remove the bowl from the saucepan. Sift in the flour and fold into the eggs with the hot water. Pour the mixture into the prepared tin and bake in the preheated oven for 8–10 minutes, or until golden and set.

**3** Transfer the sponge to a sheet of baking paper. Peel off the lining paper and roll up the sponge tightly along with the baking paper. Wrap in a tea towel and cool until completely cooled.

**4** Mix the fromage frais and almond essence together in a bowl. Leave the mixture to chill in the refrigerator until required. Wash, hull and slice the strawberries.

**5** Unroll the sponge, spread the fromage frais mixture over the sponge and sprinkle with the sliced strawberries. Roll the sponge up again and transfer to a serving plate. Sprinkle with almonds, lightly dust with icing sugar and serve.

# CHOCOLATE CHIP
## BROWNIES

**MAKES 12**

225 g/8 oz butter, softened, plus extra
   for greasing
150 g/5½ oz plain chocolate, broken into
   pieces
225 g/8 oz self-raising flour

125 g/4½ oz caster sugar
4 eggs, beaten
75 g/2¾ oz pistachio nuts, chopped
100 g/3½ oz white chocolate, roughly
   chopped
icing sugar, for dusting

**1** Preheat the oven to 180°C/350°F/Gas Mark 4. Grease a 23-cm/9-inch square baking tin and line with baking paper.

**2** Place the chocolate and softened butter in a heatproof bowl set over a saucepan of simmering water. Stir until melted, then leave to cool slightly.

**3** Sift the flour into a separate bowl and stir in the caster sugar.

**4** Stir the beaten eggs into the chocolate mixture, then pour the mixture into the flour and sugar and beat well. Stir in the pistachio nuts and white chocolate, then pour the mixture into the tin, using a palette knife to spread it evenly.

**5** Bake in the preheated oven for 30–35 minutes, or until firm to the touch around the edges. Leave to cool in the tin for 20 minutes. Turn out onto a wire rack. Dust with icing sugar and leave to cool completely. Cut into 12 pieces and serve.

# NUTTY FLAPJACKS

**MAKES 16**
115 g/4 oz butter, plus extra for greasing
200 g/7 oz rolled oats
115 g/4 oz chopped hazelnuts

55 g/2 oz plain flour
2 tbsp golden syrup
85 g/3 oz light muscovado sugar

**GRANDMA'S TIPS**

*These are very handy for lunch boxes or to take along on a picnic. Honey can be used instead of golden syrup and some dried fruit, such as apricots or cranberries, can be added for colour and flavour.*

1  Preheat the oven to 180°C/350°F/Gas Mark 4, then grease a 23-cm/9-inch square ovenproof dish or cake tin. Place the rolled oats, chopped hazelnuts and flour in a large mixing bowl and stir together.

2  Place the butter, syrup and sugar in a saucepan over a low heat and stir until melted. Pour onto the dry ingredients and mix well. Turn the mixture into the prepared ovenproof dish and smooth the surface with the back of a spoon.

3  Bake in the oven for 20–25 minutes, or until golden and firm to the touch. Mark into 16 pieces and leave to cool in the tin. When completely cooled, cut through with a sharp knife and remove from the tin.

# LEMON BUTTERFLY
## CAKES

**MAKES 12**
115 g/4 oz self-raising flour
½ tsp baking powder
115 g/4 oz butter, softened
115 g/4 oz caster sugar
2 eggs, beaten
finely grated rind of ½ lemon

2–4 tbsp milk
icing sugar, for dusting

**for the filling**
55 g/2 oz butter
115 g/4 oz icing sugar
1 tbsp lemon juice

**GRANDMA'S TIPS**

*Cupcakes are always a favourite for children's parties. You can use multi-coloured paper cases to make them look even more attractive. A whole strawberry, raspberry or glacé cherry can be popped on top to decorate.*

**1** Preheat the oven to 190°C/375°F/Gas Mark 5. Place 12 paper cases in a bun tin. Sift the flour and baking powder into a bowl. Add the butter, sugar, eggs, lemon rind and enough milk to give a medium-soft consistency. Beat the mixture thoroughly until smooth, then divide among the paper cases and bake in the preheated oven for 15–20 minutes, or until well risen and golden. Transfer to wire racks to cool.

**2** To make the filling, place the butter in a bowl. Sift in the icing sugar and add the lemon juice. Beat well until smooth and creamy. When the cakes are completely cooled, use a sharp-pointed vegetable knife to cut a circle from the top of each cake, then cut each circle in half.

**3** Spoon a little buttercream into the centre of each cake and press the 2 semi-circular pieces into it to resemble wings. Dust the cakes with sifted icing sugar before serving.

# BLUEBERRY MUFFINS

**MAKES 10–12**
250 g/9 oz plain white flour
1 tsp baking powder
pinch of salt
100 g/3½ oz demerara sugar, plus
  1 tbsp for sprinkling

1 egg, beaten
225 ml/8 fl oz milk
55 g/2 oz unsalted butter, melted
125 g/4½ oz small fresh blueberries

**1** Preheat the oven to 180°C/350°F/Gas Mark 4. Line a 12-hole muffin tin with paper cases. Sift the flour, baking powder and salt into a large bowl and stir in the sugar.

**2** Add the beaten egg, milk and melted butter to the dry ingredients and stir in lightly until just combined – do not overmix. Carefully fold in the blueberries.

**3** Spoon the mixture into the paper cases, taking care not to overfill, and sprinkle with the remaining sugar.

**4** Bake in the preheated oven for 25–30 minutes until golden brown and firm. Transfer to a wire rack to cool a little.

# SCONES

**MAKES 10–12**
450 g/1 lb plain flour, plus extra
  for dusting
½ tsp salt
2 tsp baking powder
55 g/2 oz butter

2 tbsp caster sugar
250 ml/9 fl oz milk
3 tbsp milk, for glazing
strawberry jam and clotted cream,
  to serve

**GRANDMA'S TIPS**

*These delicious scones are at their
best straight from the oven. You
can also add 55 g/2 oz dried
mixed fruit to the mixture. For
savoury scones to serve with soup,
add 55 g/2 oz grated cheese to
the mix and omit the sugar.*

**1** Preheat the oven to 220°C/425°F/Gas Mark 7.

**2** Sift the flour, salt and baking powder into a bowl. Rub in the butter until the mixture resembles breadcrumbs. Stir in the sugar.

**3** Make a well in the centre and pour in the milk. Stir in using a palette knife and make a soft dough.

4 Turn the mixture onto a floured surface and lightly flatten the dough until it is of an even thickness, about 1 cm/½ inch. Don't be heavy-handed, scones need a light touch.

**5** Use a 6-cm/2½-inch pastry cutter to cut out the scones and place on the baking tray.

**6** Glaze with a little milk and bake for 10–12 minutes, until golden and well risen.

**7** Cool on a wire rack and serve freshly baked with strawberry jam and clotted cream.

# SHORTBREAD

**MAKES 8**
115 g/4 oz butter, cut into small pieces,
    plus extra for greasing
175 g/6 oz plain flour, plus extra for
    dusting

pinch of salt
55 g/2 oz caster sugar, plus extra
    for dusting

**GRANDMA'S TIPS**

*To give shortbread a bit more texture, replace 55 g/2 oz of the flour with semolina, which will give it a more granular, slightly gritty texture.*

**1** Preheat the oven to 150°C/300°F/Gas Mark 2.

**2** Grease a 20-cm/8-inch fluted cake tin or flan tin.

**3** Mix together the flour, salt and sugar. Rub the butter into the dry ingredients. Continue to work the mixture until it forms a soft dough. Make sure you do not overwork the shortbread or it will be tough, not crumbly as it should be.

**4** Lightly press the dough into the cake tin. If you don't have a fluted tin, roll out the dough on a lightly floured board, place on a baking tray and pinch the edges to form a scalloped pattern.

**5** Mark into 8 pieces with a knife. Prick all over with a fork and bake in the centre of the oven for 45–50 minutes until the shortbread is firm and just coloured.

**6** Allow to cool in the tin and dust with the sugar. Cut into portions and remove to a wire rack. Store in an airtight container in a cool place until needed.

# CHOCOLATE CHIP
## COOKIES

**MAKES 18**

125 g/4½ oz soft margarine, plus extra
   for greasing
175 g/6 oz plain flour
1 tsp baking powder

85 g/3 oz light muscovado sugar
5 tbsp caster sugar
½ tsp vanilla essence
1 egg
125 g/4½ oz dark chocolate chips

1  Preheat the oven to 190°C/375°F/Gas Mark 5. Lightly grease two baking trays.

2  Place all of the ingredients in a large mixing bowl and beat until well combined.

3  Place tablespoonfuls of the mixture onto the baking trays, spacing them well apart to allow for spreading during cooking.

4  Bake in the preheated oven for 10–12 minutes or until the cookies are golden brown.

5  Using a palette knife, transfer the cookies to a wire rack to cool completely before serving.

# ORANGE GINGERNUTS

**MAKES 30**

125 g/4½ oz butter, plus extra for
  greasing
350 g/12 oz self-raising flour
pinch of salt
200 g/7 oz caster sugar

I tbsp ground ginger
I tsp bicarbonate of soda
75 g/2¾ oz golden syrup
I egg, beaten
I tsp grated orange rind

**GRANDMA'S TIPS**

*You may find it easier to roll out
the dough into a log shape and
then cut into slices before placing
the gingernuts on the baking
trays.*

1 Preheat the oven to 160°C/325°F/Gas Mark 3. Lightly grease several baking trays.

2 Sieve the flour, salt, sugar, ginger and bicarbonate of soda into a large mixing bowl.

3 Heat the butter and golden syrup together in a saucepan over a very low heat until the butter has melted.

4 Leave the butter mixture to cool slightly, then pour it onto the dry ingredients.

5 Add the egg and orange rind and mix thoroughly.

6 Using your hands, carefully shape the dough into 30 even-sized balls.

7 Place the balls well apart on the prepared baking trays, then flatten them slightly with your fingers.

8 Bake in the preheated oven for 15–20 minutes, then transfer them to a wire rack to cool.

# CLASSIC OATMEAL COOKIES

**MAKES 30**

175 g/6 oz butter or margarine, plus
   extra for greasing
275 g/9½ oz demerara sugar
1 egg
4 tbsp water

1 tsp vanilla essence
375 g/13 oz rolled oats
140 g/5 oz plain flour
1 tsp salt
½ tsp bicarbonate of soda

**GRANDMA'S TIPS**

*After you've made these classic cookies once, why not vary them by substituting desiccated coconut for some of the oats? You could also add some chopped nuts, chopped glacé cherries or chocolate chips.*

**1** Preheat the oven to 350°F/180°C/Gas Mark 4 and grease a large baking sheet.

**2** Cream the butter and sugar together in a large mixing bowl. Beat in the egg, water and vanilla essence until the mixture is smooth.

**3** In a separate bowl, mix the oats, flour, salt and bicarbonate of soda. Gradually stir the oat mixture into the butter mixture until thoroughly combined.

**4** Put 30 rounded tablespoonfuls of cookie mixture onto the greased baking sheet, making sure they are well spaced. Transfer to the preheated oven and bake for 15 minutes, or until the cookies are golden brown.

**5** Remove the cookies from the oven and place on a wire rack to cool before serving.

# WHITE BREAD

**MAKES 1 LARGE LOAF**

450 g/1 lb strong white flour, plus 2 tbsp
  for dusting
1 tsp salt

7 g/¼ oz easy-blend dried yeast
1 tbsp vegetable oil or melted butter,
  plus 1 tsp for greasing
300 ml/10 fl oz warm water

**1** Mix the flour, salt and yeast together in a mixing bowl. Add the oil and water and stir well to form a soft dough.

**2** Turn the dough out onto a lightly floured board and knead well by hand for 5–7 minutes. Alternatively, use a free-standing electric mixer for this and knead the dough with the dough hook for 4–5 minutes. The dough should have a smooth appearance and feel elastic.

**3** Return the dough to the bowl, cover with clingfilm and leave to rise in a warm place for 1 hour. When it has doubled in size, turn it out onto a floured board and knead again for 30 seconds; this is known as 'knocking back'. Knead it until smooth.

**4** Shape the dough into a rectangle the length of the tin and three times the width. Grease the tin well, fold the dough into three lengthways and put it in the tin with the join underneath for a well-shaped loaf. Cover and leave to rise in a warm place for 30 minutes until it has risen well above the tin.

**5** Preheat the oven to 220°C/425°F/Gas Mark 7. Bake in the centre of the preheated oven for 25–30 minutes until firm and golden brown. Test that the loaf is cooked by tapping it on the bottom – it should sound hollow. Cool on a cooling rack for 30 minutes. Store in an airtight container in a cool place for 3–4 days.

# Index